Heinemann EXPLORE Science

Teacher's Book

New International Edition

Grade 2

Tara Lievesley, Deborah Herridge
Series editor: John Stringer

PEARSON

Pearson Education Limited is a company incorporated in England and Wales having its registered office at Edinburgh Gate, Harlow, Essex, CM20 2JE.

Registered company number: 872828

Text © Pearson Education Limited 2012
First published 2003
This edition published 2012

www.pearsonglobalschools.com

16 15 14 13 12
IMP 10 9 8 7 6 5 4 3 2 1

British Library Cataloguing in Publication Data
A catalogue record for this book is available from the British Library

ISBN 978 0 435 13363 4

Copyright notice

Edited by Janice Curry
Designed by Tech-Set Ltd, Gateshead
Original illustrations © Pearson Education Limited, 2003, 2009, 2012
Illustrated by Tech-Set Ltd, Gateshead
Cover photo/illustration © Charles McClean, Alamy Images
Printed in China (SWTC/01)

Acknowledgements
Every effort has been made to contact copyright holders of material reproduced in this book. Any omissions will be rectified in subsequent printings if notice is given to the publishers.

The publisher would like to thank the following for their kind permission to reproduce their photographs:

Cover images: Front: Alamy Images

All other images © Pearson Education

In some instances we have been unable to trace the owners of copyright material, and we would appreciate any information that would enable us to do so.

Contents

New International Edition

Introduction

Heinemann Explore Science New International Edition provides a comprehensive, easy-to-use resource written especially for the international primary classroom.

The teaching framework follows the Cambridge International Examinations Primary Science Curriculum Framework (2011), enabling you to minimize planning. The simple structure of *Heinemann Explore Science* gives you flexibility to teach the Units within a grade in the order that suits your situation.

There is one Unit for each half of a term, the final half term being for assessment and review. There are six or seven lessons in each Unit. The first lesson in each Unit is an introduction Unit and the last one is a plenary. The other lessons either focus on knowledge and understanding or on manageable, tried and tested investigation activities. The greater the opportunity for investigation, the more practical lessons there are.

Each Grade of *Heinemann Explore Science* contains these detailed teacher's notes in the *Teacher's Book*, providing all the resources you need for planning and teaching successful science lessons; an accompanying *Student Book* to bring the science topics to life for the children; a *Workbook* with activities to do at school or at home; and six *Readers* to develop students' English language skills through science. Alongside these components, digital resources available via online subscription provide an e-book version of the printed books, opportunities for independent research into the Biology, Chemistry and Physics covered in the scheme and further activities and simulations. For more information on digital resources for this course, visit www.pearsonglobalschools.com/explorescience.

This unique combination of science and ICT stimulates students and enables you to deliver enriching science lessons using today's technology.

Heinemann Explore Science and English language development

Science and language development have much in common. In both, students are frequently highly motivated. Science is a popular subject area in primary schools with students (and with teachers!), and produces interesting and engaging results. Language and science are both social activities. Students' language will not develop without co-operation and collaboration, and science is also a collaborative subject. Finally, science experiences can lead, as few other subjects do, to a desire to communicate discoveries.

When developing spoken English, remember:

- Discussion can be stimulated by working in threes. Two friends doing science may have a common and familiar way of communicating. Three extends the discussion.
- Snowball or jigsaw activities, in which groups share and exchange information, are engaging.
- Discussion before and after an investigation can clarify thoughts. Having to explain what students discovered in their investigation helps clarify thinking and improve language skills.
- Presenting results to others imposes a discipline as well as giving purpose to recording and to clear presentation.
- Reading can be developed through following instructions – including safety instructions – and using the *Student Book* and targeted *Readers*.

Students may be understandably reluctant to record their discoveries. When encouraging written recording, use a variety of recording methods.

- Writing to a structure helps to order students' thoughts.
- Annotated diagrams are an effective way of recording practical science – used by adult scientists as well as students.
- A recorded observation alone may lead to a conclusion.
- Ordering and recording whole investigations is difficult, and can often be better done to a writing framework.

Heinemann Explore Science offers and defines new vocabulary. If the words are new to you, or you have any doubts yourself about their definition, use the definitions in the glossary in the *Student Book*.

- Draw the students' attention to the new words.
- Depending on the students' age, set them to illustrate or define the words themselves. Introduce word games – matching the word to the definition.
- Make a 'Words of Science' poster or a class dictionary.
- Ask the students to use the words in context; to act them out; to guess which word you are thinking of, either by 20 questions or by giving clues.
- Use cloze procedure to place new words.

Components of the scheme

The *Heinemann Explore Science* *Teacher's Book* provides detailed guidance on teaching with the corresponding sections of the *Student Book* pages. Used alongside the electronic components, where you will find a variety of resources for planning and teaching, the *Teacher's Book* is the main starting point for any lesson. Each Unit provides approximately a half-term's worth of work – an introduction, and five or six lesson plans (each of which may be taught in a single session or across science sessions during the week), and a final review.

Each Unit introduction provides:

1   Clear background science information to support the non-specialist teacher.

2   Simple definitions of necessary scientific vocabulary.

3   A complete list of resources needed in the Unit.

4   Helpful hints on prior preparation or useful additional resources.

5   Indications of what students should already know and be able to do before starting the Unit.

6   Cross-curricular references to other subject areas.

7   A discussion question to set the scene and introduce a context for the Unit.

There are two types of lesson in *Heinemann Explore Science*. The first type focuses on knowledge and understanding objectives. These lessons contain:

1   Starter activities to initiate whole-class discussion. Questioning will enable you to establish what the students already know.

2   References to the corresponding *Student Book* pages and further information to expand on the paragraphs in the *Student Book*.

3   Safety tips to advise of specific hazards where appropriate.

4   Additional information necessary for the activities in the 'Things to do' section of the *Student Book*, plus suggestions of how to differentiate and record. Any worksheets required are cross-referenced.

5   Integrated ICT research activities using the website.

6   Further details or extra 'fun facts' to support those listed in the *Student Book*.

7   The answer to the 'I wonder...' question, with additional background explanation if necessary.

8   More activities that can be used instead of, or as well as, those in the 'Things to do' section.

9   Ideas for how students could present their work or tips for classroom displays, including referenced PowerPoint templates, provided on the website to help students.

10   An activity or series of questions to reinforce the main objectives in the plenary session, drawing the lesson to a close.

The second type of lesson offers a challenge to encourage students to use scientific enquiry skills to investigate a problem in context. These contain:

1   Starter activities to initiate whole-class discussion.

2   A challenge introduced in context, explaining what students will be investigating.

3   Safety tips advising of unique hazards where appropriate; an individual risk assessment is always recommended.

4   Further details of how to carry out the investigation, supporting the instructions in the *Student Book*.

5   Lists of materials students will need, including any to be prepared in advance.

6   Explanations of what students should be looking for, or how to keep the test fair. How best to support and extend students.

7   How to organize, record, analyse and present data collected in the investigation. Suitable tables for data recording are provided as worksheets in the *Workbook*.

8   Students are encouraged to review how well they carried out their investigation and how good their results were. Using the report provided for each investigation helps students build evaluation skills by criticizing methods and conclusions.

9   A different scenario is offered to enable students to apply what they have learned.

10   Additional activities can be used instead of, or as well as, the investigative challenge.

11 An activity or series of questions to reinforce the main objectives in the plenary session, drawing the lesson to a close.

At the end of each Unit, material is provided for an assessment and review lesson:

1 A clear summary of the knowledge and skills students have gained through the Unit, divided into three levels of attainment.

2 Explanation and expected responses to the 'Check-up' in the *Student Book*.

3 Answers to the assessment worksheets in the *Workbook*.

4 The answer to the original question posed at the beginning of the Unit.

5 A final activity completes the Unit and reviews everything they have learned.

In addition, there are six *Readers* for each Grade of the Framework. These are written to match the appropriate science for the Grade, but with close attention to language levels. Students can learn English language through science, and science through practising their English.

Note that the sixth Reader, *Health and Growth*, covers topics on human health and growth which are of interest and relevance to students of this age, but are not contained in the Cambridge Primary Curriculum Framework for this Grade.

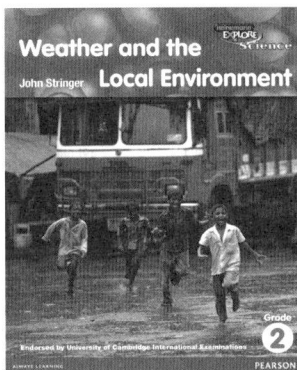

Weather and the Local Environment — John Stringer

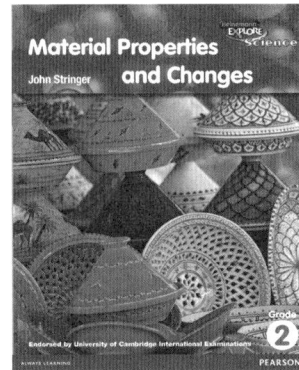

Material Properties and Changes — John Stringer

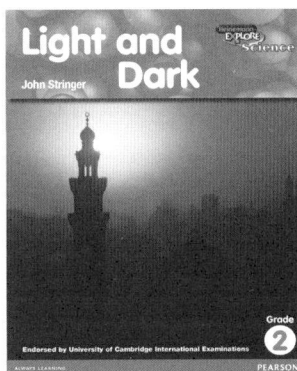

Light and Dark — John Stringer

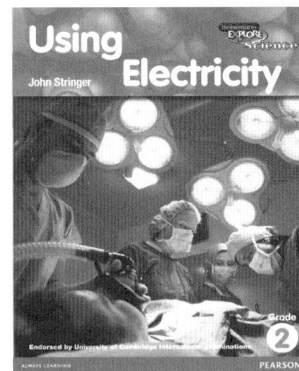

Using Electricity — John Stringer

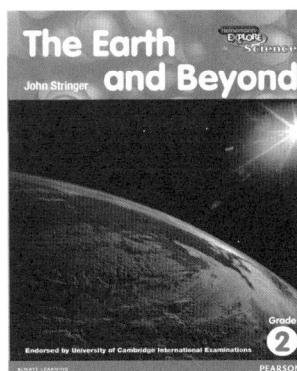

The Earth and Beyond — John Stringer

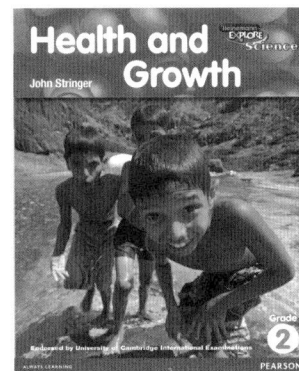

Health and Growth — John Stringer

New International Edition

Quick guide to the *Teacher's Book*

The **Heinemann Explore Science 2** *Teacher's Book* provides detailed guidance on teaching with the corresponding sections of the *Student Book* pages. Used alongside the e book, where you will find a variety of resources for planning and teaching, the *Teacher's Book* is the main starting point for any lesson. Each Unit provides approximately one half-term's worth of work and comprises an introduction, five or six lessons (each of which may be taught all at once, or across a number of science sessions during the week), plus a review.

Each Unit introduction provides:

2 A complete list of resources needed throughout the Unit.

1 Clear background science information to support the non-specialist teacher.

3 Helpful hints on prior preparation or useful resources.

4 Useful definitions of scientific vocabulary commonly misunderstood by students.

There are two types of lesson in *Heinemann Explore Science*. The first type focuses on knowledge and understanding objectives.

3 The answer to the 'I wonder...' question, with additional background explanations if necessary.

1 Starter activities initiating whole-class discussion. Questioning will enable you to find out what the students already know.

2 Safety tips warning of possible hazards where appropriate.

9 References to the corresponding *Student Book* pages and further information to expand on the paragraphs in the *Student Book*.

4 More activities that can be used instead of or as well as those in the 'Things to do' section.

8 Any additional information necessary for the activities in the 'Things to do' section of the *Student Book*, plus suggestions of how to differentiate and record.

5 Ideas for how students could present their work or tips for classroom displays.

7 Further details or extra 'fun facts' to support those listed in the *Student Book*.

6 An activity or series of questions to help reinforce the main objectives in the plenary session to draw the lesson to a close.

The second type of lesson offers a challenge to encourage students to use their scientific enquiry skills to investigate a problem in context.

1 Starter activities initiate whole-class discussion.

2 List of materials that students will need, including any that need to be prepared in advance.

3 Information on how to organize, record, analyse and present data collected in the investigation. Spreadsheet tables for recording results and exemplar data to convert into charts can be found in the *Student Book* and *Workbook*.

9 The challenge introduces the context and explains what students will be investigating.

8 Further details of how to carry out the investigation to support the instructions to the students in the *Student Book*.

4 An activity or series of questions to help reinforce the main objectives in the plenary session to draw the lesson to a close.

7 Explanations of what students should be looking for and noticing, or how they should keep the test fair. Ideas on how to support and extend students are also included.

6 Students are encouraged to review how well they carried out their investigation and how good their results were. Use the report provided for each investigation to help students build evaluation skills by criticizing methods and conclusions.

5 Present students with a different scenario to enable them to apply what they have learned.

At the end of each Unit, material is provided for an assessment and review lesson.

2 Assessment sheets can be found in the *Workbook*.

1 A clear summary of the knowledge and skills students have gained throughout the Unit.

3 A final activity completes the Unit to remind students of everything they have learned.

5 Explanation and expected responses to the 'Check-up' in the *Student Book*.

4 The answer to the original question posed at the beginning of the Unit. Discuss what the students think now in light of what they have learned.

How to use *Heinemann Explore Science*

For ease of use, ***Heinemann Explore Science*** follows the structure of the Cambridge Primary Science Curriculum Framework, 2011. ***Heinemann Explore Science*** has been written so that you can be flexible about what you teach and when.

Heinemann Explore Science is more manageable than many primary science schemes. It has a simple structure, but it also offers wide investigative and research opportunities. A range of engaging tasks is offered for each topic, including practical and research-based activities. Its clear progression and layout offers more support to less confident teachers. Integrated assessment gives indications of how to interpret levels of attainment. There is support for differentiation with suggestions for extra challenges for bright students and support for students struggling with science concepts. There is both experimental and investigative science through reliable practical investigations.

Heinemann Explore Science emphasizes: investigations; the clear use of strong vocabulary lists; building on students' ideas and addressing common misconceptions through questioning and discussion; clearly identified support and extend activities; class demonstration as a basis for some practical activities; and appropriate activities as part of students' homework. It offers flexibility of use; although Units are ordered to match the Cambridge Curriculum Framework, they can be taught in any order to suit a school's own scheme of work. This helps in mixed-age classes.

Differentiation

Within any class there will be a wide range of experience and ability. In a mixed-age class that range is further extended. This is a challenge to any teacher, and many address it through careful differentiation. Commonly, work is planned for a number of different groups (often three: high achievers, a middle range group, and students needing additional support). Teachers then allocate their resources – human and practical – to these groups to ensure the best possible outcome for everybody. This 'planning for differentiation' is demanding, and may leave feelings of dissatisfaction – 'I didn't spend long enough with

the high-fliers/slower group today', 'I hope I'm not neglecting the majority of the class'. Some teachers have similar difficulties with 'differentiation by outcome'. Less able students may be unchallenged by the assumption that they will always produce a few lines of text when others routinely write a page.

Heinemann Explore Science expects that you will need to differentiate your work, and so a range of resources is offered, any of which may stimulate particular groups. You may choose to: present an activity on an investigation table, possibly supported by an informed adult; to set out resources that students can use for creative play; or to use the *Student Book* or *Workbook* for stimulus, for direction or for recording.

The 'starting off' activities in ***Heinemann Explore Science*** invite a third form of differentiation: differentiation by presentation. This is so familiar to teachers that few recognize how effectively they use it. The way in which a topic is presented engages students, but it also enables you to assess their prior knowledge. Because of its practical nature, students who may not shine in other subjects will often contribute more in science. Students who are able in every respect may still surprise you with their knowledge, but this 'knowledge' needs to be probed carefully – a superficial knowledge may lack the depth of understanding on which new science learning can be built.

That's why ***Heinemann Explore Science*** includes a number of exemplar questions to elicit current understanding – whether it is insecure, or even whether students have misconceptions that need gently challenging. It is when you group the students and set the tasks that you 'differentiate by presentation' – an unconscious and instinctive skill that results in different groups busily engaged with differing levels of support and monitoring.

Level statements to help you identify at which level students are working are provided in this *Teacher's Book*, for each Unit. These are also provided at the back of the *Student Book* for discussion and as checklists to enable self-assessment by students.

Heinemann Explore Science contains a wide range of ideas for interaction that includes things to do, questions to ask and resources to support learning. Your professional role is in the effective deployment of those resources.

The Heinemann Explore Science website

This provides a full range of editable planning materials, generic writing frames and presentation templates to support students in recording and presenting their work.

The website also provides digital e-book versions of all the *Readers* for each Grade and for the *Student Book* and *Workbook*, so that worksheets can be downloaded and printed if needed.

Using ICT for research

Students should develop their research skills using a variety of secondary sources. Throughout the *Student Book*, students are given opportunities to use ICT to research the answers to questions related to the topic of the lesson. At the end of each Unit, a more open question with reference only to the appropriate area of study is introduced to encourage students to develop search skills and strategies.

The Heinemann Explore Science Readers

These have been written bearing in mind the language needs of students for whom English is not a first language. Each book complements a Unit in the scheme. They offer interesting illustrations and simple, engaging text. Word count increases with higher grades. They can be used as individual readers, books to read at home, or for group reading. They can be used for vocabulary and language exercise, and there are suggestions for activities at the back of each book – from crosswords to team games.

Used alongside the other components of the scheme, they offer opportunities for developing science and language, hand-in-hand.

Health and safety issues

Primary science is a very safe activity, but that does not mean that you should not consider health and safety issues when you plan, or that you should feel unsupported, either. *Heinemann Explore Science* highlights specific safety issues in lessons when appropriate, and you should also engage in your own risk assessment and

take appropriate precautions. This should not be demanding; it involves looking at your students, your circumstances and support staff, and ensuring that you have noted, minimized and if necessary recorded any apparent hazards. It is essential to share this risk assessment with other adults in the classroom.

Every adult on the school site should be familiar with the school's Health and Safety Policy, and especially how it reflects on their responsibilities. They should know the location and proper use of safety equipment. All adults have a responsibility for their own safety, and that of their students in school, whatever their age. This is a responsibility you share with others. Teaching assistants, for example, are often responsible for small groups of students doing practical activities – their supervision may be vital where a hazard has been recognized, for example, when using a cooker. Working with a small group like this offers opportunities not just for realistic but negative teaching ('Don't touch that – it's hot!') but also for positive modelling of safe behaviour ('Now how should I pick this up?')

You can give a very positive image of health and safety issues by performing a routine risk assessment while planning an activity, and encouraging students to make their own assessment of risk, and take their own precautions. Engaging students in safety planning helps them to understand the importance of not taking risks. If students are simply told what is safe without explanation, they are less likely to take it as seriously as when they are themselves involved in safety planning.

Here are a few general common-sense reminders:

Food: Eating and drinking is forbidden in school science labs, but some of primary science is concerned with food – science activities may require students to eat, but only with your permission. Fingers do get sucked, and foods are tempting. Ensure that guidelines on 'what to eat' are clear and take into account both ethnicity, custom, parental wishes and allergies.

Present the best practice in food handling: the cleaning and/or covering of tables, and the use of cooking utensils kept only for this purpose. Students should know not to enter the food area

New International Edition

unless they are in the practical group (mark or point out an area that can only be entered with clean hands and wearing an apron). Protective clothing not only keeps the students' clothes clean but also prevents food contamination. It should be kept solely for food use. PVC aprons or smocks (coveralls) can be cleaned by wiping with an antibacterial cleaner. Pull-on sleeves can be worn with aprons. Washable aprons should be hot washed at least once a term.

Laminated plastic tables are ideal. Wooden tables (or damaged laminated tables) should be covered with clean plastic tablecloths kept specifically for food. Older students can use antibacterial cleaners such as Dettox after an initial thorough clean by an adult. Spray or wipe all food preparation surfaces including chopping boards with the antibacterial cleaner, wipe with a clean cloth and leave to dry before using.

Nobody – student or adult – should work with food if they are unwell, including sickness, diarrhoea, colds, coughs and other infections. Cuts must be covered with a clean waterproof dressing – blue plasters show up if they drop into food! Supervise students washing hands before food work, or after using the toilet. Provide colourless, perfume-free liquid soap and running water. If a hot air dryer is not available, provide disposable paper towels or paper roller towels. Discourage students from touching their face, hair or other parts of their body, and from coughing or sneezing over food.

Electricity: Teach students about the dangers of mains electricity. Students live with electricity and refusing them experience of it is comparable to not teaching them road safety rules for fear of traffic accidents. Mains electricity has a far greater 'push' round the circuit than battery electricity. It is this greater push that kills. The human body is not a good conductor of electricity, but it conducts electricity far better when wet. Work with low-voltage 'battery' electricity is not risky.

Forces: Many activities in science (and technology) put students at risk because little thought is given to possible outcomes. What will happen if the elastic band snaps, the bag breaks, or the liquid spills? Students may take unnecessary risks too, by not using basic science equipment (eye protection, a cutting board or bench hook) that could keep them safe. Testing-to-breaking-point activities in topics like Forces can be

dangerous unless students have considered the consequences of breakage.

Animals: The key factor is the welfare of both students and animals. The learning outcome is an understanding of animal welfare and a positive educational experience of (say) a small mammal. It's important to ensure that none of the students has an allergy to animal fur. If you introduce family pets, it's unlikely that they are used to being surrounded by a group of excited students.

Introduce any animal to a group/class yourself. Talk about them, drawing out what the students know, and what they think about how the animal might behave. Students empathize with small animals, and will understand that they could be easily frightened.

The adult should handle the animal throughout the group activity. Students could ask their questions first, and then take it in turns to stroke the animal at the end, which reduces the chances that students will go rubbing their eyes or sucking their fingers afterwards! Stroking the back of a mammal's head is a useful lesson in how to calm an animal. After their experience, they should wash their hands again, under supervision.

General advice: Younger students can be expected to be able to control risks to themselves and others. They commonly know what is dangerous. Classroom accidents are frequently the result of students forgetting what is sensible because they are caught up in an activity, especially if it is exciting science!

Essential safety advice is contained in a book from the Association for Science Education called *'Be Safe!'* and every teacher should be aware of it and its contents. *Be Safe!* is available from The Association for Science Education, College Lane, Hatfield, Herts. AL10 9AA, UK

www.ase.org.uk *Be Safe!* ISBN: 978 0 86357 426 9

CLEAPSS is the advisory service for health and safety in science education. CLEAPSS offers informative publications, a staffed helpline, and a members' website. It is an essential source of science safety knowledge.

www.cleapss.org.uk

Curriculum structure of *Heinemann Explore Science*

Heinemann Explore Science has been very carefully structured to ensure a progressive development in the students using the course, both of scientific process skills and also of knowledge and understanding. This complements the approach taken in the Cambridge Primary Science Curriculum Framework.

The development of scientific process skills throughout the complete course is shown in this skills ladder:

Heinemann Explore Science Science Skills Ladder

Skills Domain	Year 1 Children have opportunities:	Year 2 Children have opportunities:	Year 3 Children have opportunities:	Year 4 Children have opportunities:	Year 5 Children have opportunities:	Year 6 Children have opportunities:
1. **Ideas and evidence in science**	to collect evidence to try and answer a question	to collect evidence to try and answer a question	to collect evidence in a variety of contexts to answer a question or test an idea	to collect evidence in a variety of contexts to test an idea or prediction based on their scientific knowledge and understanding	to consider how scientists have combined evidence from observation and measurement with creative thinking to suggest new ideas and explanations for phenomena	to consider how scientists have combined evidence from observation and measurement with creative thinking to suggest new ideas and explanations for phenomena
2. **Investigative skills** **Planning investigative work**	to test ideas suggested to them and say what they think will happen	to suggest some ideas and questions based on simple knowledge and say how they might find out about them; to say what they think might happen; and to think about and discuss whether comparisons and tests are fair or unfair	in a variety of contexts, to suggest questions and ideas and how to test them; to make predictions about what will happen; to think about how to collect sufficient evidence in some contexts; and to consider what makes a test unfair or evidence sufficient and, with help, plan fair tests	to suggest questions that can be tested and make predictions about what will happen, some of which are based on scientific knowledge; to design a fair test or plan how to collect sufficient evidence; and, in some contexts, to choose what apparatus to use and what to measure	to make predictions of what will happen based on scientific knowledge and understanding, and suggest how to test these; to use knowledge and understanding to plan how to carry out a fair test or how to collect sufficient evidence to test an idea; and to identify factors that need to be taken into consideration in different contexts	to decide how to turn ideas into a form that can be tested and, where appropriate, to make predictions using scientific knowledge and understanding; to identify factors that are relevant to a particular situation; to choose what evidence to collect to investigate a question, ensuring the evidence is sufficient; and to choose what equipment to use

New International Edition

Curriculum structure of *Heinemann Explore Science*

Heinemann Explore Science Science Skills Ladder

Skills Domain	Year 1 Children have opportunities:	Year 2 Children have opportunities:	Year 3 Children have opportunities:	Year 4 Children have opportunities:	Year 5 Children have opportunities:	Year 6 Children have opportunities:
3. Obtaining and presenting evidence		to make observations using appropriate senses; to make some measurements of length using standard and non-standard measures; and to present some findings in simple tables and block graphs	to make observations and comparisons; to measure length, volume of liquid and time in standard measures using simple measuring equipment effectively; and to present results in drawing bar charts and tables	to make observations and comparisons of relevant features in a variety of contexts; to make measurements of temperature, time and force as well as measurements of length; to begin to think about why measurements of length should be repeated; and to present results in bar charts and tables	to make relevant observations; to consolidate measurement of volume, temperature, time and length; to measure pulse rate; to think about why observations and measurements should be repeated; and to present results in bar charts and line graphs	to make a variety of relevant observations and measurements using simple apparatus correctly; to decide when observations and measurements need to be checked, by repeating, to give more reliable data; and to use tables, bar charts and line graphs to present results
4. Considering evidence and approach	to communicate observations orally, in drawing, by labelling and in simple writing; to make simple comparisons and groupings that relate to differences and similarities between living things and objects; in some cases to say what their observations show, and whether it was what they expected; and to draw simple conclusions and explain what they did	to make simple comparisons, identifying similarities and differences between living things, objects and events; to say what results show; to say whether their predictions were supported; in some cases to use knowledge to explain what was found out and to draw conclusions; and to explain what they did	to draw conclusions from results and begin to use scientific knowledge to suggest explanations for them; and to make generalizations and begin to identify simple patterns in results presented in tables	to identify simple trends and patterns in results presented in tables, charts and graphs and to suggest explanations for some of these; to explain what the evidence shows and whether it supports any predictions made; and to link the evidence to scientific knowledge and understanding in some contexts	to decide whether results support any prediction; to begin to evaluate repeated results; to recognize and make predictions from patterns in data and suggest explanations for these using scientific knowledge and understanding; to interpret data and think about whether it is sufficient to draw conclusions; and to draw conclusions indicating whether these match any prediction made	to make comparisons; to evaluate repeated results; to identify patterns in results and results that do not appear to fit the pattern; to use results to draw conclusions and to make further predictions; to suggest and evaluate explanations for these predictions using scientific knowledge and understanding; and to say whether the evidence supports any prediction made

Heinemann Explore Science Curriculum Matching Chart for Grade 2

This chart shows where all of the topics and Learning Outcomes specified in the Cambridge Primary Science Curriculum Framework are covered in the *Heinemann Explore Science* course.

Learning Objectives	*Student Book* coverage	Supporting coverage in *Teacher's Book* or *Workbook*
Scientific enquiry		
Scientific enquiry: Ideas and evidence		
Collect evidence by making observations when trying to answer a science question.	Unit 1: Living things in the environment • Let's explore! pp.2–3 • Home sweet home pp.4–5 • Grouping animals pp.6–7 • Caring for our environment pp.8–9 • The weather pp.10–11	*Teacher's Book* 2, pp.16–31
	Unit 2: Materials • What are rocks? pp.14–15 • Hard as nails? pp.16–17 • Natural or not? pp.18–19 • All change! pp.20–1 • Heating up pp.22–3 • Disappearing acts pp.24–5	*Teacher's Book* 2, pp.32–49
	Unit 3: Light and dark • Source of light pp.28–9 • Our Sun pp.30–1 • Using light pp.32–3 • Shady shadows pp.34–5 • Exploring shadows pp.36–7 • Changing shadows pp.38–9	*Teacher's Book* 2, pp.50–67
	Unit 4: Electricity • Bright sparks pp.42–3 • What is a circuit? pp.44–5 • What? No electricity? pp.46–7 • Making models pp.48–9 • Circuit pictures pp.50–1 • Attention seekers pp.52–3	*Teacher's Book* 2, pp.68–85
	Unit 5: Earth and beyond • Spinning around pp.58–9 • Moving shadows pp.60–1 • Happy Birthday Earth pp.62–3 • Night and day pp.64–5	*Teacher's Book* 2, pp.86–101
Use first-hand experience, e.g. observe melting ice.	Unit 1: Living things in the environment • Grouping animals pp.6–7 • The weather pp.10–11	*Teacher's Book* 2, pp.16–31
	Unit 2: Materials • Hard as nails? pp.16–17 • Natural or not? pp.18–19 • All change! pp.20–1 • Disappearing acts pp.24–5	*Teacher's Book* 2, pp.32–49
	Unit 3: Light and dark • Source of light pp.28–9 • Using light pp.32–3 • Shady shadows pp.34–5 • Exploring shadows pp.36–7 • Changing shadows pp.38–9	*Teacher's Book* 2, pp.50–67
	Unit 4: Electricity • Bright sparks pp.42–3 • What is a circuit? pp.44–5 • What? No electricity? pp.46–7 • Making models pp.48–9 • Circuit pictures pp.50–1 • Attention seekers pp.52–3	*Teacher's Book* 2, pp.68–85
	Unit 5: Earth and beyond • A galaxy far away pp.56–7 • Spinning around pp.58–9 • Night and day pp.64–5	*Teacher's Book* 2, pp.86–101

Use simple information sources.	Unit 1: Living things in the environment • Let's explore! pp.2–3 • Home sweet home pp.4–5 • Grouping animals pp.6–7 • Caring for our environment pp.8–9 • The weather pp.10–11	*Teacher's Book* 2, pp.16–31
	Unit 2: Materials • What are rocks? pp.14–15 • Natural or not? pp.18–91 • All change! pp.20–1 • Heating up pp.22–3	*Teacher's Book* 2, pp.32–49
	Unit 3: Light and dark • Source of light pp.28–9 • Using light pp.32–3 • Shady shadows pp.34–5 • Changing shadows pp.38–9	*Teacher's Book* 2, pp.50–67
	Unit 4: Electricity • Bright sparks pp.42–3 • What? No electricity? pp.46–7 • Circuit pictures pp.50–1 • Attention seekers pp.52–3	*Teacher's Book* 2, pp.68–85
	Unit 5: Earth and beyond • A galaxy far away pp.56–7 • Spinning around pp.58–9 • Moving shadows pp.60–1 • Night and day pp.64–5	*Teacher's Book* 2, pp.86–101

Scientific enquiry: Plan investigative work

Ask questions and suggest ways to answer them.	Unit 1: Living things in the environment • Let's explore! pp.2–3 • Home sweet home pp.4–5 • Grouping animals pp.6–7 • Caring for our environment pp.8–9 • The weather pp.10–11	*Teacher's Book* 2, pp.16–31
	Unit 2: Materials • What are rocks? pp.14–15 • Hard as nails? pp.16–17 • Natural or not? pp.18–19 • All change! pp.20–1 • Heating up pp.22–3 • Disappearing acts pp.24–5	*Teacher's Book* 2, pp.32–49
	Unit 3: Light and dark • Source of light pp.28–9 • Our Sun pp.30–1 • Using light pp.32–3 • Shady shadows pp.34–5 • Exploring shadows pp.36–7 • Changing shadows pp.38–9	*Teacher's Book* 2, pp.50–67
	Unit 4: Electricity • Bright sparks pp.42–3 • What is a circuit? pp.44–5 • What? No electricity? pp.46–7 • Making models pp.48–9 • Circuit pictures pp.50–1 • Attention seekers pp.52–3	*Teacher's Book* 2, pp.68–85
	Unit 5: Earth and beyond • A galaxy far away pp.56–7 • Spinning around pp.58–9 • Moving shadows pp.60–1 • Happy Birthday Earth pp.62–3 • Night and day pp.64–5	*Teacher's Book* 2, pp.86–101
Predict what will happen before deciding what to do.	Unit 2: Materials • Hard as nails? pp.16–17 • Disappearing acts pp.24–5	*Teacher's Book* 2, pp.32–49
	Unit 3: Light and dark • Exploring shadows pp.36–7	*Teacher's Book* 2, pp.50–67

	Unit 4: Electricity • What is a circuit? pp.44–5 • Attention seekers pp.52–3	*Teacher's Book* 2, pp.68–85
Recognize that a test or comparison may be unfair.	Unit 2: Materials • Disappearing acts pp.24–5 Unit 3: Light and dark • Exploring shadows pp.36–7	*Teacher's Book* 2, pp.32–49 *Teacher's Book* 2, pp.50–67

Scientific enquiry: Obtain and present evidence

Make suggestions for collecting evidence.	Unit 1: Living things in the environment • The weather pp.10-11 Unit 3: Light and dark • Light and dark p.27 Unit 5: Earth and beyond • Earth and beyond p.55	*Teacher's Book* 2, pp.16-31 *Teacher's Book* 2, pp.50-67 *Teacher's Book* 2, pp.86-101
Talk about risks and how to avoid danger.	Unit 4: Electricity • Bright sparks pp.42–3 Unit 5: Earth and beyond • Moving shadows pp.60–1	*Teacher's Book* 2, pp.68–85 *Teacher's Book* 2, pp.86–101
Make and record observations.	Unit 1: Living things in the environment • Let's explore! pp.2–3 • The weather pp.10–11 Unit 2: Materials • Disappearing acts pp.24–5 Unit 3: Light and dark • Exploring shadows pp.36–7	*Teacher's Book* 2, pp.16–31 *Teacher's Book* 2, pp.32–49 *Teacher's Book* 2, pp.50–67
Use a variety of ways to tell others what happened.	Unit 1: Living things in the environment • Let's explore! p.3 • Grouping animals p.7 Unit 2: Materials • Natural or not? p.19 • Disappearing acts p.24 Unit 3: Light and dark • Exploring shadows p.36 Unit 4: Electricity • Circuit pictures p.51	*Teacher's Book* 2, pp.16-31 *Teacher's Book* 2, pp.32-49 *Teacher's Book* 2, pp.50-67 *Teacher's Book* 2, pp.68-85

Scientific enquiry: Consider evidence and approach

Make comparisons.	Unit 4: Electricity • What is a circuit? pp.44–5	*Teacher's Book* 2, pp.68–85
Identify simple patterns and associations.	Unit 1: Living things in the environment • The weather pp.10–11 Unit 4: Electricity • What is a circuit? pp.44–5	*Teacher's Book* 2, pp.16–31 *Teacher's Book* 2, pp.68–85
Talk about predictions (orally and in text), the outcome and why this happened.	Unit 2: Materials • Hard as nails? p.17 • Disappearing acts p.25 Unit 3: Light and dark • Exploring shadows p.37 Unit 4: Electricity • What is a circuit? p.45 • Making models p.49	*Teacher's Book* 2, pp.32-49 *Teacher's Book* 2, pp.50-67 *Teacher's Book* 2, pp.68-85
Review and explain what happened.	Unit 1: Living things in the environment • Unit 1: Review p.12 Unit 2: Materials • Unit 2: Review p.26 Unit 3: Light and dark • Unit 3: Review p.40	*Teacher's Book* 2, pp.16–31 *Workbook* 2, p.12 *Teacher's Book*k 2, pp.32–49 *Workbook* 2, p.20 *Teacher's Book* 2, pp.50–67 *Workbook* 2, pp.29–30

13

	Unit 4: Electricity • Unit 4: Review p.54 Unit 5: Earth and beyond • Unit 5: Review p.66	*Teacher's Book* 2, pp.68–85 *Workbook* 2, p.43 *Teacher's Book* 2, pp.86–101 *Workbook* 2, p.51
Biology		
Biology: Living things in their environment		
Identify similarities and differences between local environments and know about some of the ways in which these affect the animals and plants that are found there.	Unit 1: Living things in the environment • Let's explore! pp.2–3 • Grouping animals pp.6–7	*Teacher's Book* 2, pp.16–31 *Workbook* 2, pp.1–8
Understand ways to care for the environment. Secondary sources can be used.	Unit 1: Living things in the environment • Caring for our environment pp.8–9	*Teacher's Book* 2, pp.16–31 *Workbook* 2, p.10
Observe and talk about their observation of the weather, recording reports of weather data.	Unit 1: Living things in the environment • The weather pp.10–11	*Teacher's Book* 2, pp.16–31 *Workbook* 2, p.11
Chemistry		
Chemistry: Material properties		
Recognize some types of rocks and the uses of different rocks.	Unit 2: Materials • What are rocks? pp.14–15	*Teacher's Book* 2, pp.32–49 *Workbook* 2, pp.13–14
Know that some materials occur naturally and others are man–made.	Unit 2: Materials • Natural or not? pp.18–19	*Teacher's Book* 2, pp32–49 *Workbook* 2, pp.13, 15–16
Chemistry: Material changes		
Know how the shapes of some materials can be changed by squashing, bending, twisting and/or stretching.	Unit 2: Materials • All change! pp.20–1	*Teacher's Book* 2, pp.32–49 *Workbook* 2, p.17
Explore and describe the way some everyday materials change when they are heated or cooled.	Unit 2: Materials • Heating up pp.22–3	*Teacher's Book* 2, pp.32–49
Recognize that some materials can dissolve in water.	Unit 2: Materials • Disappearing acts pp.24–5	*Teacher's Book* 2, pp.32–49 *Workbook* 2, p.19
Physics		
Physics: Light and dark		
Identify different light sources including the Sun.	Unit 3: Light and dark • Source of light pp.28–9 • Our Sun pp.30–1	*Teacher's Book* 2, pp.50–67 *Workbook* 2, pp.21, 24
Know that darkness is the absence of light.	Unit 3: Light and dark • Using light pp.32–3	*Teacher's Book* 2, pp.50–67
Be able to identify shadows.	Unit 3: Light and dark • Shady shadows pp34–5 • Exploring shadows pp36–7 • Changing shadows pp38–9	*Teacher's Book* 2, pp.50–67 *Workbook* 2, pp.25–28
Physics: Electricity		
Recognize the components of simple circuits involving cells (batteries).	Unit 4: Electricity • What is a circuit? pp44–5	*Teacher's Book* 2, pp.68–85 *Workbook* 2, pp.36–37, 40
Know how a switch can be used to break a circuit.	Unit 4: Electricity • Making models pp48–9 • Circuit pictures pp50–1	*Teacher's Book* 1, pp.87–106
Physics: The Earth and beyond		
Explore how the Sun *appears* to move during the day and how shadows change	Unit 5: Earth and beyond • Spinning around pp58–9 • Moving shadows pp60–1	*Teacher's Book* 2, pp.86–101 *Workbook* 2, pp.46–7
Model how the spin of the Earth leads to day and night, e.g. with different-sized balls and a torch.	Unit 5: Earth and beyond • Night and day pp64–5	*Teacher's Book* 2, pp.86–101 *Workbook* 2, p.50

Resources for *Heinemann Explore Science* Grade 2

Science equipment and durable items

aerosol cans
bells
bulb holders
bulbs
buzzers
collection of electrical appliances
compass
cooker
crocodile clips
digital camera
fish tank

freezer
fridge
globe
hand lenses
lanterns
light source (overhead projector light or strong torch)
magnifying glasses
map of the world
measuring tapes
metal nail file

metal nails
mirrors
small electric motors
overhead projector
pictures of electrical appliances
springs
switches
torches
wire

Consumables and items locally available

acrylic fabric
air fresheners
aluminium foil
balloons
batteries
beach ball
beads
beakers
bicarbonate of soda
biscuits
black paper
blackout material
bread
bubble wrap
butter
cake cases
candle moulds
candles
card
cardboard boxes
cardboard tubes
caterpillars
cellophane
chocolate
clay
clay flowerpots
clear plastic bottles
clear plastic cups
coins
corrugated cardboard
cotton
Crayola
desk lamp
doll's house furniture
double cream

felt
flour
food colouring
frogspawn
fur and fake fur
glass baubles
glass jars
glue
gravy powder
ice cubes
J–cloth
jelly
jugs
kettle
kitchen paper
large white sheet
leather belts
lemonade
lemons
lolly sticks
marshmallows
milk
mirror card
muslin
natural and artificial sponges
oil
old sunglasses
oranges
paints
pans
pasta
PE hoops
peas
pebbles
plant misting sprayer

plaster of Paris
plastic belts
plastic flowerpots
plastic gloves
plastic jar with lid
plastic spoons
Plasticine
porridge
pulses
raisins
rice-based cereal
rocks and stones
salt
saucers
sequins
spoons
sterile potting compost
straws
sugar
sugars
syrup
tights
tinsel
tracing paper
trowel
vinegar
washing up liquid
waterproof fabric
wax crayons
wires
wooden spoons
wool
yeast

New International Edition

Unit 1: Living things in the environment

The objectives for this Unit are that students should be able to:

- Identify similarities and differences between local environments and know about some of the ways in which these affect animals and plants that are found there.

- Understand some ways in which humans impact on the local and worldwide environment and suggest ways to care for the environment.

- Observe and talk about the weather, recording reports of weather data.

- Collect evidence by making observations when trying to answer a science question.

- Make and record observations.

SB p.1   Science background

Even in the most unpromising of locations, your local environment supports a rich variety of plants and animal life. In this Unit, students are encouraged to take a closer look at the plants and animals around them and to consider why different plants and animals are found in different environments.

From the Sahara desert to the North Pole, the bottom of the Pacific Ocean to the top of the Himalayas, life is everywhere. Anywhere a living organism makes its home is called its habitat. A habitat is a plant's or animal's living address.

The physical conditions and weather conditions of any area define what a habitat or an environment is like – the temperature, amount of rainfall or water, shelter and so on. Some environments change little over time but others may change drastically with the changing seasons.

Survival

Living things can only survive in a local habitat if they have characteristics that allow them to do so; they do not suddenly equip themselves with new characteristics because they choose to live in a particular habitat – this is a talent peculiar to humans. Students often misunderstand the cause and effect relationship here. For example, if we want to live in a cold climate, we may wear heavy coats and thick boots; animals don't have that

choice. Students may say, 'The polar bear grows thick fur so it can live in the snow,' But they really should say, 'Only polar bears with thick coats could survive in those cold temperatures.'

The same is true for plants. Only those with characteristics that allow them to survive the local conditions will live there. For instance, in a dry, sunny environment like a desert, only plants with small leaves or spines can survive the extreme lack of water.

Your local area may not accommodate a wide range of habitats, but you may still be able to observe differences between wet and dry, shady and light, cultivated and wild areas. You will even be able to find differences between North and South facing walls of a building.

Caring for the environment

In this Unit, students are introduced to some ideas of how changing environmental conditions can affect the nature of what can survive there. Students are encouraged to take positive action to care for their local environment. They are also introduced to weather as an environmental factor and how to observe and record various weather phenomena.

Animals in the classroom

Keeping animals in the classroom is an exciting and rewarding experience for students. However, out of their normal habitat some will die, no matter how hard we try to replicate natural conditions. Refer to your school guidelines for advice.

If you are keeping insects, put fresh leaves in the tank every day and mist the inside with water to stop the atmosphere getting too dry.

Hatching ducklings or chicks is possible with an incubator; however it can be quite tricky and students may well get upset if some of the chicks die or are born with deformities.

All captive animals should be returned to their original habitats once you have finished studying them. Hatched chicks may be welcomed at a local farm!

Language

environment	everything around us; all the conditions, influences and physical landscape surrounding a living thing

grow	get bigger by adding to yourself
habitat	the 'natural home' of a plant or an animal; the place in which a plant or animal lives
hibernate	spending the winter in an inactive (dormant) state
insect	an invertebrate characterized by a three-sectioned body and three pairs of legs, e.g. fly, bee, ant
larva	the eating stage of an inset that develops from an egg
life cycle	the stages living things go through from fertilization to death
meteorologist	A scientist who studies the weather
migrate	to move from one region to another according to the change of seasons
minibeasts	used to describe insects and other small invertebrates
organism	collective name for any living thing, whether it is a plant or an animal
pupa	the intermediate stage between larva and adult stages
weather	climatic and environmental conditions caused by the interaction of water, wind and heat from the Sun

The Words to learn list on page 1 of the *Student Book* can be used to make a classroom display.

Resources

- *Weather and the Local Environment* Reader.
- Digital camera
- Hand lenses and magnifying glasses
- Trowel
- Large white sheet
- Fish tank
- Plant misting sprayer
- Map or globe
- Sterile potting compost
- Empty plastic drinks bottles
- Pictures or photographs of different habitats
- Black paper
- Pictures of plants and animals
- PE hoops
- Packaging from hamburger meal
- Pictures of extinct or endangered animals
- Picture of cityscape
- Tracing paper
- Map of the world
- Frogspawn or caterpillars
- Muslin
- Cardboard tubes
- Lolly sticks

Bright ideas

The use of digital cameras as recording equipment is useful to help students quickly make a record of an animal or plant in the environment.

Ready-made habitats for animals (either for outdoor or indoor use) can be purchased online. Be aware however that differences in climate may restrict the times of year when these can be successfully used and schools should only grow animals native to the environment, particularly if they intend to release them into the wild.

Even though students at this stage may not be creating identification keys, they are useful tools for the teacher to have around and to refer to for information on unfamiliar plants and animals.

Other investigations you might like to try include:

- Which part of the school has the most living things in it? Which has the fewest? Why?
- Are all insects the same?
- Which is the best environment for ants?
- What is lichen and can I find any growing in or near the school?
- What are fungi and where would I find them?
- Why can some plants be harmful?
- Do the same birds come to the school all year round?
- Record the weather over the course of several weeks.

Knowledge check

- Students will have already encountered the idea that plants, humans and other animals are alive and that they grow (by adding to themselves).
- Most students will know and be able to name a variety of plants and animals living in their local environment. They will also know that flowering plants produce seeds that can grow into new plants. Students should be able to point out the seed within a fruit.

Skills check

Students need to:

- be able to describe what they observe as they explore the environment.
- in studying the weather, be able to record observations in a table.
- with help, be able to use measurements they make of weather to draw simple conclusions.
- know some comparative expression, e.g. hotter than, wetter than.

Links to other subjects

Litcracy: Rcad storics and pocms about plants, seeds and animals growing and changing.

Write a story about what it would be like to live in a very hot or very cold place.

Read and use captions and labels. Write captions and labels for their own work.

Follow simple instructions, make simple recordings in tables.

Make simple lists and write simple instructions.

Write a letter to a newspaper about developing your school as a nature habitat.

Develop your home corner into a role-play safari park to develop language about plants, animals, their habitats and how to care for them.

Numeracy: Opportunities for counting up to, and beyond, ten.

Read, write and order numbers.

Make height comparisons and compare numbers of leaves, petals, wings or legs.

Measure volumes of water in non-standard units.

Measure time in days and weeks and use calendars as recording devices.

Talk about the shapes we see in plants – What shape are the petals?

Talk about the patterns we see on animals, e.g. the symmetry of a butterfly's wing.

Other subjects:

Bring **Art and Design** into the science of the natural world:

Students can draw, paint or sculpt plants, make prints and casts from leaves or bark, press flowers and use seeds, twigs and bark as collage materials.

Encourage students to design their own living environments – What would be a good habitat for a person? How is this different from a good habitat for a bird? What do both need?

Let's find out...

The Unit opens with this question:

Why do we have nature reserves?

This question is included to start students thinking about the impermanence of some habitats, particularly because of the influence of humans. Young students often feel there is nothing they can do to stop the destruction of habitats, but here you can discuss how individuals can make a difference by collectively deciding to protect special environments and the animals and plants in them by the creation of nature reserves, to keep living things safe from harm.

Unit 1: Living things in the environment – Let's explore!

The objectives for this lesson are that students should be able to:

- Know that there are different animals and plants in their local environment

- Know that not all parts of the environment are the same

- Name common plants and animals and state where they can be found

- Understand that some animals and plants are only found in some places

- Make simple observations and communicate ideas

- Record observations in a table provided for them.

SB p.2 | *Starter*

Brainstorm students' understanding of 'animal' and 'plant'. Try to list an animal and a plant for each letter of the alphabet. Highlight those that you would expect to find locally. *Which have we left out? Why wouldn't we find them around here?*

Talk about plants and animals that the students may have seen at home. *Are they all welcome? Are there any animals that we wouldn't like to share our houses with?*

SB pp.2–3 | *Explain*

What is the environment?

Students will be introduced to two new words which have very similar meanings: habitat and environment, which should be clarified and re-clarified throughout.

The environment is everything around us; all the conditions, influences and physical landscape surrounding a living thing. A habitat is a particular place where a plant or animals lives within a particular environment. So for example, a habitat for a frog may be in a pond which is within a forest environment.

Students may not identify trees or grasses as plants, nor recognize small creatures as animals.

Remind them not to disturb any animals or damage plants when working outside.

> ⚠ Wash hands after handling soil, animals and plants. Watch out for plant allergies and avoid sap on skin.

Things to do | WS 1&2

Sharing an environment

Animals and plants do not live in isolation, they share the environment and a habitat. Sometimes we share our habitat with plants or animals that we may think of as unwelcome, such as weeds in gardens or bugs, pests and insects in our homes.

Go on a local bug hunt in a safe fertile area. *Why should we avoid disturbing animals and damaging plants?*

Ask students to draw the animals they find and complete WS 1. Use a digital camera to record examples and their locations. Concentrate on where plants are growing and where there are animals, e.g. beetles under stones, snails in damp areas, spiders in shrubs or on walls, birds on lawns and in trees. Remember to inspect the underside of leaves. Stress the importance of good hygiene when handling plants and particularly soil. Ask students to choose one of the animals or plants they have found and look very closely at it and draw it in detail on WS2.

Leave damp logs and plant pots or some old carpet tiles in a quiet, shady outdoor corner if you have one. Keep the area damp. You will attract some small invertebrates in time.

If there are earthworms in your local soil, make a wormery in a fish tank with some damp soil, leaves, twigs and small pieces of fruit. Cover it with black sugar paper or store it in a dark place. Keep the atmosphere moist by spraying it daily. Record which shaped leaves the worms prefer to pull into their burrows. *Are there any plants that the worms don't like? Why?*

Differentiation

More able students could collect indirect evidence for the presence of animals. Holes in leaves indicate that a caterpillar has been eating, broken snail shells may be evidence of carnivorous birds. Look out for footprints, snail trails, spiders' webs, or nests.

Less able students can sketch an environment and stick pictures of animals in appropriate places. *Why did you choose that place?*

Dig deeper

Together, make a map of your school grounds showing the numbers and location of plants and animals – in flowerbeds, wall cracks, trees, under stones, etc. Agree that plants and animals are found in particular places. Show pictures of plants and animals generally found in your area. Ask where you would expect to find them around school. Let students write labels for the map, e.g. 'We found this centipede under a stone'.

Ask the students if they found anything in the school grounds that they consider to be dangerous to animals or plants. You might suggest rubbish lying around that small animals might get caught in or choke on, broken glass or sharp objects or plastic bags or packaging that animals could get tangled in.

Discuss possible hidden dangers to animals and plants in the environment such as careless disposal of household or industrial waste, pollution, new buildings that cast shade on previously sunny areas where plants could grow, etc.

Did you know?

We have only explored and discovered a fraction of the world's living plants and animals and many species we have discovered have yet to be named as there are so many of them! As scientists explore the deep oceans, more and more remarkable animals are being found.

I wonder...

Life exists in even the most unpromising places, in the deep ocean or caves where no light can penetrate, in the frozen soil in the tundra. Some life even exists on or inside other creatures and we call these things parasites. Maybe the most unusual place that life exists hasn't even been explored yet.

Other ideas

Use stories and songs about animals and plants to reinforce and extend subject knowledge of the names of plants and animals. Include stories from different parts of the world and talk about the different environments in the world. Also include stories closer to home that include descriptions of rural and urban environments.

Draw an imaginary environment and the animals and plants within it. Give your made-up animals and plants names.

Play 'Twenty Questions', the game where the students have to ask questions which can only be answered by 'yes' or 'no' to decide on the identity of a creature.

Presentation

WS 2

Make a large display of a school 'Ark'. You can use the pictures students have already drawn on WS2. Place within the ark pictures and labels of animals and plants that live around the school and would need to be 'rescued' if the world was in danger as in traditional flood stories.

Plenary

Make a magnetic fishing game using paper clips and magnets, substituting pictures of plants and animals for fish. Can students correctly place their 'catches' on a plan of your school or a locality map?

Return any creatures you have collected to their natural habitat.

New International Edition

Unit 1: Living things in the environment – Home sweet home

The objectives for this lesson are that students should be able to:

- Know what a habitat is and give examples
- Know that there are differences between habitats and the plants and animals found there
- Suggest reasons for particular organisms living in particular habitats
- Make simple observations and communicate ideas
- Make comparisons between animals and plants in different habitats.

SB p.4 | *Starter*

Discuss what a home is. *Where do you live – in a house, flat, in the country or the town? Do these homes have anything in common?* (shelter, warmth). *What sort of things do we do at home?* (eat, sleep, grow, feel safe). Explain that the scientific name for a home is 'habitat'.

SB pp.4–5 | *Explain*

Where I live

A habitat is a plant or animal's home. Common habitats that the students may be familiar with are woods and trees, ponds, rock pools, rivers and ponds, soil and so on. Students need to understand that there are differences between habitats and the plants and animals found there. Try to develop an understanding of the reasons for particular organisms being in particular habitats.

Students may believe that animals 'choose' a place to live rather than understanding that animals survive in a place because they have the right adaptations.

Remind students not to disturb animals or damage any plants that they find.

> ⚠ Exercise extreme caution when near water. Check that water sites are not affected by Weil's disease, bilharzia or other water-borne diseases.

WS 3 | *Things to do*

The wrong place

Look at *Student Book* page 4. Compare the habitats. *How are plants and animals adapted to living there?*

Create some pictures of mismatched animals and habitats, e.g. a lion at the seashore, a fish in a desert, an oak tree at the bottom of the sea, etc. *What is wrong? Where should the animals/plants live? Why?* Explain that animals are suited to where they live.

Investigate two contrasting areas: the rich variety of life in forests, ponds or seashores, contrasted with the immediate school environment. In urban areas, investigate walls, gardens and (with careful supervision) water. Let students predict and then discover animals and plants in each area. Let them draw and write about the differences they find. *Why are these habitats home to different things? Did you find the animals and plants you expected?*

Make fact files of habitats and their inhabitants. Create a scrubland, forest or water habitat using collected materials from your field trip. Use a fish tank with sufficient fresh food and water for animals to survive. Return animals to their original habitats when investigations are complete.

Create a 'habitat picture' of a detailed landscape. Make 'lift the flap' stones, leaves, logs, soil surface, etc. to reveal creatures you might find beneath them.

Together, pretend you are an 'animal or plant estate agency'. Create advertisements for 'the ideal habitat' for different animals and plants. Discuss what your animal or plant would need if it were to move from its current home. *Which habitats would be completely unsuitable? Why?*

Investigate hibernation and migration of animals in cooler countries.

Look around the school grounds for animal homes. They may not be so spectacular – small holes for insects and worms, perhaps – but they give the idea that most animals have a home offering shelter and a degree of security. You could introduce the word 'habitat' to describe an animal's home.

Ask students to complete WS 3.

Differentiation

More able students can research global habitats and the wildlife that inhabits deserts, tundra, rainforests and oceans. Stick pictures of recognizable animals in the centre of sheets of paper. Ask students to draw the animal's habitat around it.

Give less able students a picture of a plant or animal. Ask them what they need to survive.

Dig deeper

Explain that some animals need to change their home as the seasons change and their food supply may become scarce. Many birds, for example, travel to or from warmer places to store up food for the winter months. We call this movement 'migration'.

Did you know?

Hibernating animals deal with a lack of food in the colder months by slowing their metabolism down so much that they behave as if they are in a deep sleep; their breathing slows and their body temperature drops. Usually a hibernating animal will prepare for this period by eating large amounts of food to see it through its hibernation period.

Desert animals like the jerboa go into a sleepy state, which is called aestivating, when the weather is intensely hot. It seals its burrow with a plug of earth and reduces its activity until the conditions are more comfortable.

I wonder...

The only animal that can effectively live 'anywhere' is man. Humans have learned to modify and change hostile environments to enable them to live there successfully. We can make clothes; build houses and fires to keep us warm where animals cannot do this. We have developed cooling systems and shelter to safeguard us from harsh sunlight so we can live in very warm places too.

Other ideas

WS 4

Students can use WS4 to add plants and animals to a rainforest environment.

Play 'twenty questions' – one student pretends to be a particular animal or plant and the others ask questions about its habitat to guess its identity.

How many animal homes can they name? (web, nest, burrow, set, house, etc.).

'Who lives in a house like this...?' Describe a habitat and students deduce from your clues which animal home you are describing.

Presentation

With pictures of 'habitats' and of plants and animals (taken around school with a digital camera), ask students to match the organism to the habitat and explain their reasons. Include creatures or plants that students have not yet encountered.

Plenary

Talk about being responsible for looking after our environment and for keeping it safe for ourselves and everything else that lives in it. Resolve to look after the school environment and protect the habitats of the plants and animals in it.

New International Edition

Unit 1: Living things in the environment – Grouping animals

Some work in this area (for example, simple keys) goes beyond the Cambridge Curriculum Framework for Grade 2, but offers opportunities to extend and engage more able students. The objectives for this lesson are that students should be able to:

- Know that there are similarities and differences between plants (and animals)

- Know that living things are all organisms

- Know that living things can be grouped in different ways

- Know that humans belong to the animal group

- Make observations and recognize simple characteristics of animals and plants

- Choose criteria for sorting organisms

- Present and explain findings.

SB p.6   *Starter*

Give each student a picture of either an animal or a plant (avoid difficult organisms and deliberately leave out humans to begin with) and put out three PE hoops labelled 'animal', 'plant' and 'not sure'. *Why did you place that picture in that group?* Look at all the animals in the animal group. *Do they share any characteristics?* Now look at all the plants. *Are there any features that all of the plants have in common?* Photograph, keep or note the outcome to review learning later.

Sometimes minibeasts get a 'bad press'; talk about how some insects can be very useful to us – honey produced by honey bees is an important source of food in Arabia and bees also help to pollinate crops as they collect nectar and pollen from flowers, for example.

SB pp.6–7   *Explain*   WS 5

Same and different

Students will know that some things in the environment are living and others are not. They will already know that plants and animals are living organisms, and will have classified these by their habitat, environment or other basic features. Work through WS5 to remind them of this.

Now introduce them to the more systematic sorting methods scientists use to classify the immense variety of life on Earth. For your information, the Linnaean system of classifying the natural world works by placing organisms into groups according to their characteristics. Some characteristics are easy to determine such as colour, but others may relate to lifestyle (e.g. giving birth to live young) and so may be more difficult for students to grasp. Scientists continually revise and refine the Linnaean system as more information is revealed about individual animals. Looking at differences and similarities helps us to identify which group organisms belong to.

Are humans animals?

Scientists classify humans as part of the group of animals known as mammals, i.e. those animals which breathe through lungs and are 'warm-blooded' – they can keep a steady internal body temperature unrelated to the outside temperature; mammals give birth to live young, which they suckle with milk; they have hair or fur on their bodies. Examples include gazelles, dogs, whales, rats and dolphins. Although a whale lives in a marine habitat, it is a mammal and gives birth to live young. It is more closely related to a rabbit than to a fish!

⚠ Wash hands after handling soil, animals and plants. Watch out for plant allergies and avoid getting sap on skin.

Things to do   WS 6&7

Animals

Look at *Student Book* page 7. Do the students know the names of any of these creatures? *Have you seen any around school?* Explain that these animals are called 'minibeasts' because they are very small. Look together at the tally chart of Class 2's results and ask the students to complete the graph on WS6.

Look at the insects on WS7 and explain their different parts. Now contrast insects with arachnids, like spiders and scorpions. *Who can spot differences between insects and spiders?* Look at the remaining pictures. *Can they join the insect or spider group or do they need different groups?* Can students suggest features shared by different insects, spiders and others?

Explain that minibeasts can be sorted into groups based on shared characteristics. Show students photographs of new minibeasts. *Which group would you put this minibeast in? Why?* Talk about the differences between them and between minibeasts and farm or domestic animals.

Discuss the different habitats where minibeasts might be found. Ask the students, in groups, to count and classify the minibeasts they find around the school using a tally chart.

Back in class, they should compile a whole class block graph of 'Life Around School'. Discuss what the chart can tell us and other ways of showing the information.

Differentiation

More able students may make additional graphs and charts for each location around school or for different collections of living things in the environment.

Support other students by suggesting criteria for sorting, e.g. number of legs, wings, etc.

Dig deeper

WS
8

The first criterion for grouping animals is whether or not they have a backbone – those that do are called vertebrates, and those without a backbone are called invertebrates. It can be difficult for students to decide whether or not an animal has a backbone; it may help them if you talk about animals with skeletons on the inside, outside or without a skeleton at all.

There are five groups or vertebrates, defined by different characteristics: fish, amphibians, reptiles, birds and mammals.

The invertebrates have many more subdivisions but the two major ones that the students are likely to experience are:

- **Insects**: these have three body parts (head, abdomen and thorax) and three pairs of legs; some, but not all, have wings.

- **Arachnids**: these have two body parts and four pairs of legs; examples include spiders and scorpions.

The important thing for students to remember is that animals are classified together into small groups because of common characteristics, and these small groups can be joined together to make bigger groups again because of shared features. With more able students, you can consider using WS8 to show how a simple key can help with classification.

Did you know?

Some minibeasts go through two stages of metamorphosis; others three. Use pictures to show the changes of caterpillar to butterfly for example. Children may be familiar with some insects that change appearance completely as they grow such as bees, wasps and ants and others such as termites or locusts go through what is called 'incomplete metamorphosis' from egg to nymph stages and then after several 'moults' where the nymph sheds its skin, to adult.

Emphasize that metamorphosis is rare. Most animals do not change their appearance completely; they just get bigger as they get older.

I wonder...

Spiders and scorpions form a group of animals called arachnids. Arachnids have eight jointed legs where insects have six. Scorpions are nocturnal and among the first animals to have existed on Earth.

Other ideas

WS
9

Play the Snakes and Ladders Game on WS9.

Play a game of charades to act out and try and identify common animals (you could even try plants such as trees or cactus).

Read some 'Just So' stories which aim to explain in a humorous way why animals have the features they do.

Presentation

Make a pop-up puppet butterfly and chrysalis. Decorate a cardboard tube as a chrysalis and stick a paper butterfly onto a lolly stick. Insert it in the tube and make it pop up from the top, revealing colourful wings.

Create a dance piece based on metamorphosis and present it in an assembly.

Plenary

Talk about how there is a place in the world for every living thing – those that are like us and those that are very different.

Ask students to imagine what it would feel like to shrink to the size of a beetle. *What would it be like living in a hole in the ground or a crack in the wall?*

25

Unit 1: Living things in the environment – Caring for our environment

The objectives for this lesson are that students should be able to:

- Know that animals live in habitats that are special to them
- Recognize that humans can damage habitats and give examples
- Understand how living things and their habitats need protecting
- Suggest ways to protect endangered animals, plants or habitats
- Use secondary sources to research.

SB p.8   **Starter**

Bring in the packaging for a children's meal from a hamburger restaurant. Do the students like this type of food?

Now ask the students to imagine a world without cows. *What do we get from a cow that is useful to us?* Students are likely to suggest milk (and from milk we get cheese, butter, yoghurt, milk to make milkshakes, cream and ice cream) Also, we get meat from cows and leather too. If there were suddenly no cows we would have no burger chain meals. But do animals just suddenly disappear?

SB pp.8–9   **Explain**

Dead as a Dodo

Show a picture of a Dodo bird. Tell the students that these creatures have been extinct for over 300 years. Native to the island of Mauritius in the Indian Ocean, they had no natural predators but they fell prey to hungry visiting sailors and their dogs. The Dodo is now extinct which means there are no living Dodos left in the world, either in their natural habitat or in zoos.

Animals in danger

Extinction is a real prospect for many animals and plants in the world today. Living things can come under threat of extinction through man preying upon them as food and reducing their numbers e.g. North Sea Cod fish. Plants can be endangered by deforestation or land clearance or by the introduction of more vigorous invasive alien species into their habitat. Animals may bc cndangcrcd by loss of habitat too or loss of food supply in general or, in the case of for example the rhino, the desire of poachers to kill and acquire their horns.

Introduce the idea that animals and plants living in the same habitat are linked together by their surroundings. The animals may eat the plants to survive so if the plants die out or are replaced then those animals will no longer have an abundant food supply and will be at risk. We look at food chains and feeding relationships in more detail in later Grades but it is worth emphasizing that nothing living in the world exists in isolation of everything else.

> ⚠ If choosing to work outside, exercise extreme caution when near water. Check that water sites are not affected by Weil's disease or bilharzia. Remind students of the need for good personal hygiene and hand washing after handling plants, animals or soil.

Things to do

In my backyard

Look at all of the data you have collected so far on what animals and plants you have living around your school.

Consider what might happen if all the trees, shrubs and lawns were dug up and concrete or tarmac laid down to make more car parking spaces. *What if a local pond was filled in and built over? What do you think would happen to the plants and animals?*

Help students to understand that even relatively small changes in an environment can cause large changes to the wildlife that lives there.

People tend to have an urge to make their mark on the environment, to change and mould the landscape and use the resources of the Earth for their own needs. Give students photocopied pictures of city landscapes. Give them tracing paper to lay over the pictures so that the detail shows through. Ask them to draw the same landscape but without any signs that humans have been there. *What are the things that would stay the same?* (rivers, coasts, cliffs, etc.) *What would change?*

Make sure that you offer a balanced view – not all of man's influences are destructive and people do need places to live and work too.

In groups and using secondary source material choose one environment to investigate; for example the Amazonian rainforest, coral reefs, the Arctic, the African savannah grasslands or a more local environment to you such as an estuary, seashore, wadi or wetland area.

Create an information leaflet on your chosen area with facts about the plants and animals that live there. *Are any of them under threat at the moment? If so from what and could anything be done to save them?*

Together, write a letter from an endangered animal you have researched to the people of the world. Explain why the animal is endangered and what humans could do to help protect it.

Differentiation

More able students can research less well-known global habitats and the wildlife that inhabits them or choose to focus on a local area. Also, more able students may be able to understand the vital role that plants play in the environment and choose to focus on these less assuming organisms rather than their more famous animal neighbours.

Give less able students pictures of endangered animals to place on a world map to show that this is a worldwide problem.

Dig deeper

Use the Internet to find out about the Worldwide Fund for Nature or other similar conservation organizations. Discuss the value of such organizations and the importance of their work. You can find them at http://www.wwf.org

Did you know?

Ecology is the science of the environment. 'Eco' means home, habitat or environment and 'ology' is an area of science. So ecology is the scientific study of the relationships between living things and their environment.

I wonder...

WS 10

Students often feel that they alone cannot do much to halt environmental change

on a global scale but can be quite empowered to 'start small' at a local level. Something as simple as regular 'litter picking' around school not only improves the look of the environment but removes possible risks to wildlife which may for example become caught up in plastic bags or ties. Students can complete WS10 to share two things they might do to help the environment.

> ⚠ Make sure your grounds are free from sharp objects or needles which may cut students and encourage them to wear gloves whilst litter picking.

Other ideas

Plant a wildlife garden with areas left to grow wild and untended so natural wildlife will be encouraged.

Start a poster campaign for 'Small Changes – Big Differences'. *If we all ate one hamburger fewer each week, how much forest would be saved from being cleared to use the land for cattle grazing?*

Presentation

Make a frieze around the classroom filled with all of the resources humans draw from nature and the environment e.g. crops, fruits, building materials, oil and petrol, water, timber and stone, materials for our clothes and shoes, paper from trees and so on. Consider what our world would be like without these things.

Plenary

Talk about the importance of protecting the environment. Include a short reading attributed to Chief Seattle (the chief of the Suquamish American Indians).

In 1851 he delivered a speech on the importance of the environment to us and future generations, in response to a US government proposal for the Indians to sell two million acres of land for $150,000, at 7.5 cents an acre. His response is considered to be one of the most beautiful and profound statements on the environment ever made. More information can be found at www.halcyon.com/arborhts/chiefsea. html

27

Unit 1: Living things in the environment – The weather

The objectives for this lesson are that students should be able to:

- Know that different places in the world have different weather and be able to describe different weather conditions

- Understand that some scientists observe and measure the weather

- Discover by observing and recording what their local weather is like

- Discover that by studying patterns in the weather we can predict what it will be like in the future

- Make simple records.

SB p.10 — Starter

'Red sky at night, shepherd's delight; red sky at morning, shepherd's warning'. *Have you ever heard that rhyme?* It's an old English saying that the colour of the sky at various times of the day is a good clue to the approaching weather.

Other sayings and traditions are that a ring or halo around the Moon is a sign that rain is coming or that 'rain before seven, fine before eleven' means that early morning rain will be short lived. Do the students know any other sayings or traditions to predict the weather? How reliable do they think these old sayings are?

Find examples of extreme weather and discuss how phenomena such as tsunamis and drought can impact on the environment.

SB pp.10–11 — Explain

Whatever the weather

Explain that in most places in the world the weather changes either over the course of a year or over days, but sometimes it can change several times a day. The kind of weather we experience is due to the influence of three factors: heat from the Sun which gives us different temperatures, the movement of air which gives us wind and the level of water in the air which can either fall as rain or snow or other 'precipitation' or can be suspended as fog or humidity.

Introduce vocabulary to describe different weather conditions and ensure that the students are familiar with the terms even if they are unfamiliar with the weather.

Extreme weather

Students in the context of this Unit are already aware of the damage that can occur to habitats and the environment due to human activity (building, deforestation, pollution etc.) but the weather can cause damage too.

Extreme weather events have been in the news over recent years. Tsunamis and droughts have been particularly damaging as have the hurricanes that struck the southern United States.

> ⚠ Be a safe scientist. If choosing to work outside, make sure that students never look directly at the Sun as it could damage their eyesight.

Things to do

Tomorrow's weather

Explain that scientists have been interested in the weather from the earliest of times. People needed to know when to expect sunshine, rain and cold weather as these things were important for them to know when they were planting crops. The weather is still important for us, for farmers and in our everyday lives.

Play a recording of your local weather forecast. Explain that the scientist who prepares the forecast is called a meteorologist. The meteorologist is not necessarily the same person as the weather presenter.

What sorts of conditions were mentioned in the weather forecast? How might the students gather information on hours of sunshine, rainfall, wind? Collect suggestions.

Measuring the winds

Students can investigate the scale invented to judge wind strength by British Admiral Sir Francis Beaufort. Beaufort was a naval admiral and he invented this scale in the days when all ships were powered by sail. It was important to measure the force of the wind. Beaufort divided his wind scale into 13 parts from 'force 0' which is total calm to 'force 12' which is hurricane strength. Students could measure wind strength on this scale for their weather records or invent their own weather scale. Think about a scale to represent sunshine levels or how hot the day is.

Students will learn to read thermometers later in their school career and it is not necessary to introduce fine measures of temperature at this stage. Talk about relative states of being cold, warm and hot.

Differentiation

More able students can research less well-known weather scientists such as Luke Howard who introduced the first scientific classification system for clouds. A display of annotated photographs or chalk drawings of cloud types makes a good display feature.

Give less able students pictures of different weather photographs as postcards. Ask them to choose one to describe as if they were writing a postcard home and they were describing this type of weather to their friends and family.

Dig deeper

Modern meteorologists use weather satellites now to gather information about the world's weather. Pictures are sent back to weather stations from space and measurements are collected from weather stations all over the world to be collated to form weather maps and forecasts.

Did you know?

Yuma, Arizona, has sunshine for 90% of the time it is possible to have sun in Arizona. Students can use secondary sources to discover other weather facts such as the wettest place in the world, the driest place in Africa or the Americas, the most rain that fell in a single day etc.

I wonder...

In Europe there are folk traditions that the state of certain plants can give clues about the weather. For example, seaweed becomes very brittle and dry when the air is dry but when there is moisture in the air it becomes supple and shiny. Similarly pine cones open up when the air is dry to release their seed. When the air is moist they close up again.

Other ideas

WS 11

Students can make their own weather map of their area with symbols of their own devising. Take turns in presenting the day's weather and record the performance on video.

Students could complete a diary of weather for a week, using symbols, on WS11.

Gather holiday brochures or information from books and the Internet on the weather in popular holiday destinations. Discuss which the students prefer and why.

Presentation

Take photographs of a feature in the outdoor environment at the same time every day from the same position for several days or weeks. Arrange them in chronological order. *How does the scene change with the changing weather?*

Plenary

Weather is something we take for granted, especially if we live in a place where the weather patterns are fairly stable. Recap on what weather is and what it can do (good and bad aspects). Look at the weather data you have collected. *Can you see any patterns?* If not, you could go on collecting data.

Encourage students now to listen more attentively to weather forecasts and to make a note of how accurate they are over a period of time.

Unit 1: Living things in the environment – Unit 1 Review

The objectives for this lesson are that students should be able to:

- Check what they have learned about living things in the environment in this Unit

- Find out how they are working within the Grade 2 level.

SB p.12 **Expectations**

Students working towards Grade 2 level will:

- Describe simple features of plants and animals.

- Describe simple features of their local environment.

- Reply to straightforward questions using task-based observations.

- Follow simple directions/orders and react to teacher prompts and use simple equipment chosen by the teacher.

- Make observations and make a pertinent remark during an activity/event, and give simple (non-comparative) descriptions.

- Observe a trend but not give reasons for it.

In addition, students working within Grade 2 level will:

- Describe where plants and animals can be found.

- Describe which conditions minibeasts prefer in controlled conditions.

- Predict in simple terms what may happen but not give reasons.

- Conduct a fair test with teacher support, having already named potential variables.

- Recognize when a test may not be fair but not give reasons why.

- Use simple tables to record results.

- Spot similarities that establish a trend.

- Evaluate results in terms of prediction. With teacher help, can describe a casual relationship, but not give reasons for it.

Further to this, students working beyond Grade 2 level will also:

- Explain in simple terms that weather differs over time and by global location.

- Recognize some common features of habitats and the plants and animals found there.

- With support, plan and conduct a fair test, working out which factor is being tested.

- Support simple explanations using own observations.

- Support own observations using simple quantitative comparisons.

- Use simple equipment to measure and make relevant observations.

- With teacher support, work out what they need to measure or observe in an activity.

- With teacher help, create tables and bar charts to record results.

Check-up

Discuss the reasons why Rani might be concerned.

- Rani could be concerned about the physical dangers of animals becoming entangled in abandoned rubbish, restricting their movements or ability to eat or drink.

- There may also be pollutants in the water that we cannot see, e.g. dissolved substances which may be harmful if ingested such as fertilizers from farmers' fields.

Assessment

Use the Unit 1 Assessment on WS12 to check students' understanding of the content of the Unit. The answers are given below.

Name: _____ Date: _____

WS 12

Unit 1 assessment

1 The place an animal or plant lives is called its _____ .

2 Look at these pictures. Draw lines to connect each animal to where it lives.

f ___ b ___ s ___ b ___ g ___

3 Write the names of the animals underneath their pictures.

4 Sort the animals. How many legs does each animal have? Write two in each box.

No legs	Six legs	More than six legs
earthworm		

12   Heinemann Explore Science Grade 2

Answers

1 Habitat.

2 Fish matched to lake.
Bee matched to beehive.
Spider matched to web.

Bird matched to nest.
Gerbil matched to burrow.

3 Fish, bee, spider, bird, gerbil written under the pictures.

4 Table completed correctly.

No legs	Six legs	More than six legs
earthworm snail	beetle ant	spider centipede

The answer!

Refer back to the original question about nature reserves. The students should now be able to explain that the actions of humans can have an effect on the environment and the animals and plants within it. Equally, they should know that humans have the ability to make choices about what to do with their environment and how to create habitats, such as nature reserves, in which animals and plants can be protected. Talk about nature reserves in your local area or famous reserves such as the Kruger National Park in South Africa or Yellowstone Park in the USA.

And finally...

Have a 'Celebrate Our Environment Day' where students make a special effort to take care of their surroundings. This could include litter picking, weeding and planting in gardens or grounds or creating wildlife areas or creature feeders such as bird feeders or tables. Create a display using all of the photographs you have already taken over the course of the Unit, and have a vote on the 'favourite' animal and plant in your environment.

Unit 2: Materials

The objectives for this Unit are that students should be able to:

- Recognize some types of rocks and the uses of different rocks.

- Know that some materials occur naturally and others are artificial.

- Know how the shapes of some materials can be changed by squashing, bending, twisting and/ or stretching.

- Explore and describe the way some everyday materials change when heated or cooled.

- Recognize that some materials can dissolve in water.

- Ask questions and suggest ways to answer them.

- Collect evidence by making observations when trying to answer a science question.

- Use first-hand experiences, e.g. observe melting ice.

SB p.13 | Science background

Materials come in all shapes and sizes, with different properties and in different states. Use plenty of examples of non-sheet materials in the lessons – rocks or minerals, powders, liquids, foodstuffs and plants.

Materials exist as solids, liquids or gases and many can change from one into another, often as the temperature changes. Some changes can be reversed, others cannot. Materials can occur naturally or be made by people – artificial or synthetic materials.

Most of the materials around us have been changed from their natural state. The original raw materials may come from plants, animals, the earth, water or even the air. They are changed by chemical processes, often involving heat, into materials with special properties. Clay is baked to make bricks and pottery (something students may have experienced). Iron is heated and treated to make stronger, more flexible steel.

Natural or artificial?

It is often difficult to say if a material is natural or artificial. Some materials are obviously natural and

children can see them in their local environment – wood, sand, stone and water. Others have been processed but are still recognizably natural – wool, straw and bricks. Completely synthetic materials can be designed and created by combining raw materials in new ways. Most of these originate with oil (which is itself a natural material) – plastics such as polystyrene, polyester and nylon. Some new materials are made to look as though they are natural such as fake fur, metalized and wood-effect plastics.

Coal is a natural material. It was made from decaying plant matter which in turn was synthesized by trees from water and carbon dioxide using the energy of the Sun. So the answer to where coal comes from could, scientifically speaking, be the Earth, trees, or the Sun.

To simplify all this, concentrate on distinguishing three main groups:

- natural materials like coal, wooden twigs, cotton and wool

- processed or treated materials like bricks, paper, stainless steel or leather

- synthetic materials like plastics, nylon or polystyrene.

Changing materials

Materials can change in many ways. Some changes can be reversed, other cannot. You can change materials by changing their shape, mixing, melting, freezing, burning, dissolving, diluting, condensing, evaporating, sieving, filtering and corroding. Some 'reversible' changes are incomplete. Chocolate and butter can be melted and reformed – but both lose a little water in the process, and so are subtly changed.

When a change is reversible you can get the original material back, e.g. straightening a bent piece of wire, separating a mixture of sand and stone, or getting salt back from water by evaporation. Irreversible changes often involve the creation of new materials and include baking cakes (the ingredients cannot be recovered) or burning wood.

The physical shape of materials can be changed in many ways: by cutting, squashing (Plasticine and dough), stretching (rubber), and heating (melting butter or chocolate). Moulds are often used to create desired shapes of materials. Metal

32

can be pressed to shape; plastics can be pressed or 'sucked' into shape by a vacuum; wood can be cut and sanded.

Reversible changes

When a material changes its state from a solid to a liquid or a gas it may have very different properties but it is still the same material. It is a reversible change. Water is easy to see in all three states: as water (liquid), as ice (solid) and as water vapour or 'steam' (gas). Changes in state tend to come about because of changes in temperature. They can be summarized in the diagram below.

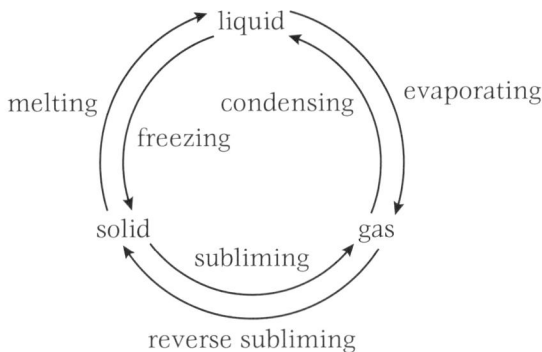

Rarely, some solids can change directly to gas and back again – a process called sublimation, not experienced in primary science, but included here for completeness. Sublimation is so rare that students are unlikely to meet it – dry ice used for stage 'smoke' is one example.

It is easy to confuse some scientific words, particularly melting and dissolving. Melting is a change of state. Dissolving is the combining of one material with another – usually a solid in a liquid. Ice cubes melt in warm water whereas sugar dissolves in tea.

Solids can hold their shape, liquids pour to take the shape of the container and always have a flat top, and gases spread through the air. Some solids can 'pour', but powders 'pile up' to form a 'peak' and liquids do not. Many gases are colourless and odourless which makes it hard to describe them. You can feel air as wind. Balloons give students a better sense that air exists and takes up space. The bubbles in a fizzy drink are a gas called carbon dioxide, which is why we can say the drinks are carbonated. Steam is the everyday word for water vapour which is the visible form of water 'gas'. True steam is the invisible gas, above boiling point,

at the spout of a kettle. In primary science, the word 'gas' can be used to describe both.

Language	
bendy	easy to push or pull out of shape
boiling	when a liquid is heated and turns to gas or vapour
*****change of state**	to change from solid to liquid, for example
*****condense**	a gas changing to a liquid
*****dilute**	reduce the strength (usually by adding water)
dissolving	a solid (or liquid) combined with a liquid
*****evaporating**	a liquid changing into a gas
fabric	a textile or cloth
freezing	a liquid changing to a solid
irreversible	cannot be changed back, permanent
magnetic	attracted to a magnet
manufactured	treated or made in some way
material	all the 'stuff' around us, solid, liquid or gas
melting	a solid changing to a liquid
mixing	combining two materials
natural	found like this in nature
properties	the qualities of materials
reversible	can be changed back
rusting	the corrosion of iron by oxygen and water
squashing	changing shape by applying a force
state	to be a solid, liquid or gas
*****synthetic**	'new' material artificially made
*****transparent**	light passes through it easily

(* technical definitions generally for teachers, not students, at this stage)

The key words to learn are given in the Words to learn list on page 13 of the *Student Book*.

Resources

- *Material Properties and Changes* Reader
- Examples of natural, processed and synthetic materials: plastic and clay flowerpots; wooden, plastic and metal spoons; natural and artificial sponges; wool and acrylic fabric; fur and fake fur; leather and plastic belts
- Modelling materials including Plasticine, clay, flour or salt dough, Crayola Model Magic™, Soft Mo™ or Fimo™ , biscuit mixture, plaster of Paris
- Old sunglasses
- Metal nails
- Stone and pebbles
- Coins
- Metal nail file
- Photos of sculptures made from different rock
- Picture of mountain landscape and lake
- Natural sheep's wool
- Woollen yarn
- Moulded plastic items (bottles, bowls)
- Items that stretch (tights, a spring)
- Corrugated cardboard
- Balloons
- Foods including milk, double cream, lemon juice, bicarbonate of soda, vinegar, jelly, chocolate, butter, bread, sugar, marshmallows, rice-based cereal, ice-pops, yeast, raisins, lemonade, pasta, pulses and porridge, oranges, lemons
- Food colouring
- Plastic gloves
- Cake cases
- A J-cloth
- Plastic jar with lid
- Wax pan
- Candle moulds
- Wax crayons
- Liquids such as oil, washing up liquid, syrup

- Aerosol cans and air fresheners
- Clear bottles
- Kitchen paper
- Ice cubes
- Waterproof fabric
- Soap bubbles
- Straws
- Saucers
- Access to a cooker, a freezer, a fridge, a kettle and a pan
- Chocolates and candy sweets of varying types including milk, white and plain chocolate, chocolate with biscuits and/or candy inclusions, candy-coated chocolates, sugar candy sweets

Bright ideas

Materials in the world that students experience tend not to exist outside the context in which they are used. Get together a collection of materials in their original state to compare with objects made from the same materials so students can see them in both forms.

Sweets and chocolates can be used to demonstrate the properties of materials. Be aware of students with diabetes.

Other ideas you might like to try:

- Explore the changes that take place when a kettle boils, as a safe teacher demonstration. Observe the 'invisible' steam at the kettle spout; the visible water vapour clouding the air; the condensed water on a cold surface like a mirror or window. Carefully collect the condensed water and show that it is still water even though it has changed in such a dramatic way.

- Demonstrate the changes that take place when it rains by making a cloud in a bag. Seal a little water in a plastic freezer bag. Tape it to the middle of a warm, sunny window. The heat will evaporate the water, which forms a cloud in the bag. The water condenses on the roof of the bag, then drips back to the bottom. It's raining indoors! Compare this with what happens in real life. If the rain only fell and the water never returned to the sky, we would run out of rain!

Knowledge check

- Students will be able to name and describe common materials and know that there are many types of materials with different characteristics.

- Students will learn that some materials are naturally occurring and some are not, and will be able to group them on this basis.

- They will find that the shape of some materials can be changed, and that heating and cooling can change the state of materials from a solid to a liquid or back again.

- Students will learn that some changes are reversible while others are not.

Skills check

Students need to:

- use observation and communication skills.

- predict outcomes and turn ideas into a form that can be tested.

- be able to carry out fair tests.

- be able to make simple measurements and to record their findings in simple tables or with words and pictures.

- be encouraged to use expressions linking cause and effect such as 'because'.

Links to other subjects

As work on materials includes items that are found around us every day, particularly food, there are good cross-subject links including:

Literacy:	Distinguish everyday from scientific language.
	Name materials.
	Develop descriptive words for the properties of materials.
	Describe similarities and differences.
	Write labels, annotate diagrams.
	Make simple lists and write simple instructions.
	Write recipes which involve changing ingredients by melting or baking.
	Creative writing.
	Poetry and drama.
	Follow simple instructions.
	Read fiction (stories and rhymes).

	Use information books.
	Investigate the biographies of the great 'fossil hunters' such as Mary Anning and in modern times, Zhao Xijin.
Numeracy:	Sort materials into groups. Use a Venn diagram for overlapping groups.
	Describe shape, using 3D shapes.
	Measure.
	Time.
	Count and order by size.
Other subjects:	The science work on changing food materials links to **Food Technology**.
	ICT links can be made by searching the Internet or using CD-ROMs.
	In **Art and Design** study the works of great sculptors and artists. What materials have they used? Have they used materials in their natural state or have they changed them? Even a study of how paint is made can turn into a study of mixing and dissolving natural and artificial pigments.
	The movement of solids, liquids and gases could become the stimulus for a **PE** or **Dance** lesson.

Let's find out...

The Unit opens with this question about Mr Silly:

Why are these not the right materials?

The objects Mr Silly uses are deliberately exaggerating the use of inappropriate materials for specific purposes. This is to get the idea across to students that we use materials with particular properties to do particular jobs for us. Many materials have more than one property; so for example, although one might want a bed to be soft, we wouldn't want it to be made out of jelly because that is too soft and without sufficient strength for support. Concrete, although strong and waterproof, is insufficiently flexible and too heavy to make effective shoes. Although students can usually identify the properties of various materials, they sometimes struggle to identify why that particular property makes a material useful for a particular job. By deliberately exaggerating inappropriate properties, students will begin to recognize properties of materials that are appropriate.

35

Unit 2: Materials – What are rocks?

The objectives for this lesson are that students should be able to:

- Know that the Earth is covered in rock

- Be able to describe some common rocks by observable features

- Recognize and name some common rocks

- Know that rocks are classified by the way they were formed

- Give some uses of common rocks.

SB p.14   *Starter*

Start your lesson with a vinegar volcano!

Cover a small pop bottle with a cone of card coloured to resemble the slopes of a volcano. Place a couple of teaspoons of sodium bicarbonate (baking soda) in the empty bottle along with some red powder paint. When you are ready, pour in a little white vinegar and watch your volcano erupt.

Explain that the students will be studying the products of volcanic eruptions and the turbulent beginning of our planet millions of years ago.

SB pp.14–15   *Explain*

Under our feet

Explain that the Earth is shaped like a ball and within that are different layers. The centre of the Earth is a solid core of iron and nickel; beyond that the outer core is liquid metal. The next layer, the mantle, is a deep layer of hot, slushy rock and covering this is the crust. The Earth's crust is made of hard rock. Sometimes the hot, molten rock from the mantle bursts through the crust and that is when we get volcanic eruptions. It's a bit like opening a can of fizzy pop. The pressure that causes the pop to spurt out is the same sort of pressure that causes volcanoes.

All rocks are made from chemicals called minerals. Each type of rock has its own chemical composition depending upon the minerals it contains. Each type of rock has a different property. Students may think that all rocks are pretty much the same and use words to describe them such as hard, heavy, dark etc. In fact many rocks are very soft, such as

talc or light like pumice and no one would describe brilliant white marble as dark. Emphasize there are lots of types of rocks, made up of different minerals, all with different colours and textures and formed a long time ago.

Ancient rocks

The Earth formed around 5,000 million years ago as a cloud of spinning gases and dust in space. Gradually the material started to clump together to form our Earth. It settled in layers – the lightest material on the outside layer and the heavier material at the centre.

Things to do   WS 13

Types of rocks

Bring in a selection of different types of chocolate – milk, plain, white, chocolate that contains raisins and biscuits or pieces of candy and chocolate that has bubbles in it. Allow the students to examine the chocolate pieces carefully and to describe what they see. Ask if the outside of the chocolate piece looks the same as the inside. Can students describe the colours, the textures? Use descriptive language to identify a 'mystery' chocolate rock – can the students guess which piece you are describing.

Explain that scientists classify rocks in the same way – by their appearance – but they also classify rocks also by the way they were made.

For your own background information, there are three main types of rock:

Igneous rocks, like granite and basalt, are made in the same sort of way that molten wax runs down the side of a candle and solidifies. Molten rock expelled from the Earth's mantle becomes solid as it cools.

Sedimentary rocks are made from tiny pieces of rock that have been worn down over time. These particles are laid down as layers of sediments, a bit like a sandwich, and then compressed into a solid mass of rock.

Metamorphic rocks are formed when other rocks are changed by heat or by pressure, a bit like mixing up ingredients for a cake and then baking it. They can be formed from either igneous or sedimentary rocks. Metamorphosis means 'change'.

Use WS13 to help students identify the properties of different rocks.

What's inside?

Rocks can provide all sorts of clues as to what life was like on Earth millions of years ago. A fossil is formed when a plant or animal dies and is covered by layers of mud or sand. As more and more layers of sand and mud lie on top of the dead plant or animal, the soft parts rot away; but sometimes the hard parts like bones or stems remain. After a long time, the chemicals in the buried bodies undergo a series of chemical changes so that eventually the bones and stems turn into something more like rock – a fossil.

Differentiation

More able students can research and categorize rock types or make a short presentation on 'How to make a rock' giving details on the three major rock types.

Give less able students the opportunity to create different movements or actions to symbolize the three types of rock – how would they act out the layered formation of sedimentary rock or the idea that igneous rock comes 'from fire'?

Dig deeper

The use of rocks is something that students can research at home as well as in school. Look around – how many examples of rocks can be seen? Some rocks may be used to build houses or roads, some are used as floors in our homes (e.g. marble or slate or stone), other rocks may be used as worktops in kitchens such as granite. In some countries rocks such as slate are used as a waterproof covering for roofs. We have cosmetic uses for rocks too – talc is a rock we use on our skin.

Did you know?

Richard Owen coined the word dinosaur and was also the founder of the Natural History Museum in London. Mounted dinosaur fossils and models are great attractions in museums all over the world. Students can research other palaeontologists

(scientists who study fossils) or the dinosaur remains they study.

I wonder...

Most homes are indeed made of rock – stone, like marble, baked clay or brick, chemically changed stone or concrete, and baked clay or tile.

Other ideas

Students can make their own fossils by pressing leaves or shells into blocks of Plasticine to make moulds then filling the moulds with plaster of Paris and turning the 'fossil' out when the plaster has set. For edible fossils, coat your clean mould with a thin layer of cooking oil and fill with melted chocolate and allow to set.

Pressed flowers on sandy coloured sugar paper can look very like fossils found in sandstone beds today.

> ⚠ Always supervise students using plaster of Paris and follow the mixing instructions given exactly. Take care not to inhale the powder and do not touch the plaster as it dries because it gives off heat. Never encase any part of your body in drying plaster of Paris.

Presentation

Draw a large outline of a house or your classroom. Fill it with pictures of things that are made from rock and used in the various rooms, e.g. salt in the kitchen, marble hallways or cutting boards in a kitchen, slate floors etc.

Plenary

Rocks are everywhere but we often do not realise that they are there. They are like history books that are 'as old as the hills', and they can tell us lots about how the Earth was made and even what animals and plants were once alive but are now no longer around.

37

Unit 2: Materials – Hard as nails?

This activity goes beyond the requirements of Grade 2 by offering one of the few practical opportunities for a scientific enquiry into rocks. The objectives for this lesson are that students should be able to:

- Carry out a simple scratch test on a selection of rocks
- Make predictions
- Make comparisons
- Make simple records of their results and draw conclusions from these
- Identify simple patterns and associations.

SB p.16   Starter

Come to class with a bag full of stones (either picked up from a beach or the surrounding area or from an educational kit). Pre-prepare an old set of sunglasses or reading glasses, the lenses of which you have previously scratched very badly and include these in the bag along with a few nails and a chocolate bar. Tip out the contents of the bag and loudly complain that you can't use the glasses ever again because they have been scratched by the stones, or was it the nails, or perhaps it was the chocolate bar?

Discuss what is the most likely object to scratch the glasses and why.

SB pp.16–17   The challenge

Read the opening conversation on page 16 of the *Student Book*. Ask students for their ideas about helping Kofi find the answer. Define what we mean by hard and soft – in this investigation the terms are relative to each other. This investigation is based on exploring the Mohs scale which ranks minerals by hardest from 1–10. Talc has a score of 0 on the scale, being the softest mineral, with diamond, the hardest being 10.

What to do

Start with all of your samples – four or five should be enough. Make sure you have a good range of hard and soft stones. Ask the students in groups to first test each sample with their fingernail. Set aside those stones scratched by the fingernail test.

Then try scratching the remaining stones with a coin – set the scratched stones aside. Next try to scratch the remaining stones with any rock not scratched by a coin.

Set these stones aside too. You should now have the stones arranged in order of soft to hard. Now try scratching the hardest stones with the nail file.

What you need

Collection of various rocks, stones or pebbles of different hardness, a coin, a metal nail file.

⚠️ Take care with sharp objects. Students should always scratch the stones in a direction away from their body to prevent accidents.

What to check

Students can double-check their results by swapping samples and testing each other's. Discuss why scientists sometimes repeat investigations lots of times.

Differentiation

There is no real need to know the names of the sample stones as they can just be labelled by number but students may enjoy finding out the names. More able students can have more samples to test and rank, taking care to be systematic in their testing. Students who struggle will only need to make a comparison of perhaps two or three samples.

What did you find?   WS 14

Look together at Kofi's results on WS14, and work through the questions.

Kofi found that chalk and soapstone scratched easily but he couldn't differentiate the other stones and thought they were equally hard.

Is this the same with your class?

Record

Make a 'cabinet of geological curiosities' with small cardboard boxes painted and glued together to make a display case for your rock samples. Label each exhibit and make an information point with facts and information about each exhibit.

Find photographs of sculptures and art works created from different rocks. Display with a sample of the rock in its uncarved state if possible near to the picture.

Did you know?

On the Mohs scale of hardness, diamond at 10 is the hardest rock we know. It is also rare and valuable. Students may not know that precious and semi-precious stones are formed in the same way as their duller companion rocks.

Now predict

Discuss Kofi's investigation to try to scratch each of his rocks with each of the other rocks. If he records his results carefully and systematically, for example in a table similar to the one on WS14, he should be able to place all six of his rocks into an order of hardness.

Can you do better?

Attempting to scratch each of the rocks with a nail file will not enable the children to put all of their rocks into an order of hardness. It will just show them where the metal of which the nail file is made, usually steel, comes in the sequence of hardness of the rocks. Steel usually has a hardness of about 7 on the Mohs scale, placing it at about the same level of hardness as granite.

Presentation

On your discovery table, place a range of objects which can change regularly (they do not have to be rocks); encourage students to arrange them in order of hardness and to make a simple version of the Mohs scale (see sample below).

Sample Mohs scale

Index Mineral	Scale	Common Objects
Diamond	10	
Corundum	9	
Topaz	8	
Quartz	7	Steel file (6.5)
Orthoclase	6	
Apatite	5	Glass (5.5)
Fluorite	4	Knife blade (5.1) Wire nail (4.5)
Calcite	3	Penny (3.5)
Gypsum	1	Fingernail (2.5)
Talc	1	

Plenary

How hard or soft a rock is can help us decide how best to use it. When we describe what something is like, we are describing its properties. Hardness or softness is a property of a rock. We wouldn't want to build our homes from rock that was too soft!

Unit 2: Materials – Natural or not?

The objectives for this lesson are that students should be able to:

- Use observation or research to identify materials and where they come from

- Know that materials come from different sources

- Discover where materials come from

- Group materials and describe their similarities and differences

- Know that materials are all different; some are natural, some are not

- Know that we change some natural materials so we can use them.

SB p.18 | **Starter**

Revisit earlier work from Grade 1 to remind students that materials come in all shapes and sizes, with different properties and in different states. Ask students to imagine, or show them a picture of a mountain, a lake, and the air around them. Here are the three states of materials: a solid mountain, a liquid lake and the air is a gas. Let students draw a concept map or spider diagram, writing words they connect to materials.

All the 'stuff' in the world around us is a type of material. Some materials are found naturally, others are artificially made. Look around you. What can students see that might be naturally occurring or artificial?

SB pp.18–19 | **Explain**

What am I?

Look at page 18 of the *Student Book*. Ask what is going on. *What is the material? Where did it come from?*

Clay is a natural product, dug from the earth. Make connections with the students' experience. They may have made clay pots or other objects in school. Take them through the stages: digging, shaping, drying (all reversible), firing (which is not), painting and glazing. The natural material is transformed to a made material. Emphasize that clay is a natural material but we change it so that we can use it.

WS 15&16

Things to do

Natural changes

Explain that although a material may come from a natural source, e.g. wool from a sheep, wood from a tree, we often process this material or change it into a form that is easier for us to use. The material is still natural but processed.

Show a selection of materials and objects made from them. *How has the material been changed so that we can use it?*

Make a clay pot! You may have access to a kiln; but there are a number of proprietary clays which can be treated (by an adult) with a special hardener.

Talk about how materials are formed (e.g. wood from trees, coal and soil from compressed plant material).

Identify natural material around the classroom, in the grounds, and from a list of words on the wall. Create a display of natural materials, or make a collage using only natural materials.

Complete WS15; students have to match the animal, plant or mineral to what it is made into or produces to make a final product.

Encourage students to sort a selection of materials into three main groups: natural materials (coal, feather, stone, wooden twig, crystals); processed materials (bricks, paper, stainless steel, leather belt); and synthetic materials (plastic bag, nylon rope, polystyrene cup).

Display the same object made from natural and artificial materials, such as a plastic and a clay flowerpot, or a wooden and plastic or metal spoon. *What are the advantages and disadvantages of each? Which would you want to use? When? Why?*

I made it myself

Explain that some materials have been made entirely by people and these are called artificial.

Look around your classroom. Ask students to sort which materials are totally natural, natural but changed or artificial? Can students sort them into groups?

Compare natural materials with artificial alternatives, such as a natural and artificial sponge, wool and acrylic fabric, fur and fake fur, leather and plastic belts. Describe all the similarities and differences between the materials. Students can make lists of natural and artificial materials on WS16.

Talk about fakes and compare them with genuine materials. They often have different properties. Can students make fakes? Let them make papier mâché jewellery or paint animal skin patterns.

Look at industries where materials are made or altered. There may be some close to school – a pottery, a bakery, a factory; find out about the manufacturing processes that change materials.

Differentiation

More able students may distinguish between materials that are living, non-living and never living.

They could use Venn diagrams to physically group materials by type or origin, using the overlap area for materials such as a wooden bat with a plastic handle.

Give less able students a picture pairs game to play with pictures of natural materials to match to objects from which they came or into which they are made, e.g. sheep and skein of wool, skein of wool and woollen clothing, clay and clay pot, leather and shoes etc.

Dig deeper

We consume many foods and drinks that contain artificial additives, chemical flavourings or colourings, but also some foods that are entirely 'fake'. Look at synthetic meat products like Quorn or synthetic sweeteners to replace sugar. *Why would we substitute a fake product for a real one? What are the advantages and disadvantages?*

Did you know?

Nylon was the first totally synthetic fibre. It was made in the 1930s by Wallace Carothers working for the Du Pont chemical company in the USA.

I wonder...

What are your clothes or possessions made from? Are they natural or not? Do the labels provide any clues? Fabrics can be difficult; many are mixed fibres, combining the properties of natural and man-made materials.

Other ideas

Invite students to create a short drama where they take on the personality of a natural material. They must describe themselves and where they come from before they announce what they are. Use music or sound effects, such as hard or soft or rustling to convey properties of materials. Students can also make props or costumes to enhance their performance.

Presentation

Make a 'washing line' of materials across your classroom. Hang up examples of clothing on the line labelled with the material from which they are made, e.g. woollen scarf, cotton shirt etc.

Plenary

Play a game to consolidate 'materials' vocabulary. Students can make a circle and select one person to stand in the centre (or this could be the teacher). The person in the centre throws a soft ball or bean bag to students around the circle who, when they catch the ball, have to shout out the name of a material (avoiding 'repeats') – if they cannot think of a new one they must sit down. The winners are the last few students standing.

Unit 2: Materials – All change!

The objectives for this lesson are that students should be able to:

- Use practical and investigative skills to explore changes in materials

- Discover that some materials can be changed

- Discover that we can change the shape of some materials by bending, twisting and stretching.

SB p.20   ***Starter***

Look at page 20 of the *Student Book*. Explain that materials can change in many ways. Some changes can be reversed, others cannot. Talk about what you can do to change different materials – students may suggest melting, mixing, squashing. Introduce other changes such as bending, twisting and stretching.

Demonstrate each type of change with appropriate safety precautions. Students can record what happened alongside the scientific word. Discuss and record which type of change is permanent.

SB pp.20–21   ***Explain***

Changing shape

Focus on changing shape. Materials that are used for modelling are designed to change shape with the application of force – moulding, shaping etc. However, some, like clay, may be permanently or irreversibly changed by heating. When they cool down they are changed forever – the clay cannot become soft and malleable again.

Focus on changing shape. Give students a range of malleable materials – Plasticine, clay, flour and water dough, salt dough, etc. Challenge them to make different shapes – long or round or twisted. *Which materials hold their shape best?* Leave the shapes to dry overnight or heat them in an oven. *How have they changed?* Extend this by making shaped biscuits. *How do they change when they are cooked?*

Reversible or not?

Other materials such as chocolate can change when heated, but when cooled they revert to the same state as before – this change is caused by heating and we call it melting, but it can be changed back by cooling so we call it a reversible change.

Be aware in your explanations that heating can both soften and harden materials, e.g. it softens chocolate but hardens clay.

Students often confuse the definitions of melting and dissolving so pay particular attention to these.

> ⚠ Be aware of possible outcomes with the stretching activities.
>
> Take appropriate precautions with any activities involving heat or cooking.

Things to do   **WS 17**

Will it change?

Look at the pictures in the *Student Book* on page 21. Discuss possible ways in which the objects or materials could be changed. Think about changing by force, by heating or cooling. Ask students how we could change the shape of non-malleable materials such as a stick or a metal bar. They may suggest breaking or melting. *Are these changes reversible?*

Use small amounts of modelling materials such as Crayola Model Magic™, Fimo™ or Soft Mo™ to make items like badges or key rings. Follow the instructions to harden them. *Can the change be reversed?*

Investigate other moulds. Push fossils or leaves into Plasticine. Use papier mâché or plaster of Paris to make moulds that will set hard. Collect a range of moulded plastic items – bottles, bowls, balls, etc. Discuss how they might be made.

Look at materials that stretch and twist: rubber, tights, elastic bands, a spring, etc. *Do they hold their shape? Why not?* Select materials to predict and then sort into two groups: those that do and do not hold their shape. Test which material is the stretchiest.

Demonstrate how changing the shape of materials often strengthens them. Fold, roll and corrugate paper. Look closely at how cardboard is corrugated.

Students can complete WS17.

Let students draw an example of objects showing each type of change, such as a rusty nail, a melting lollipop. Display the drawings alongside the glossary of words.

Differentiation

More able students can describe changes of shape using mathematical terms (I changed this circle of Plasticine into a triangle, a spiral, a square, etc.). How are similar shapes related? (e.g. an oval is a 'squashed circle').

Support less able student to help them group examples of 'changes' into those caused by heating or cooling and those caused by changing shape, squashing, squeezing or stretching.

Dig deeper

Metals can be changed by shaping them by force as in twisting wires or beating gold. They can also be heated and melted into a molten state to be poured into moulds. (The only metal which is a liquid at normal room temperature is mercury.) These changes are reversible; metals can be changed permanently by a chemical reaction that leads to rusting or oxidization or corrosion of the metal which cannot be reversed.

Did you know?

A bathroom is full of rocks, from the obvious ones like marble tiles, or porcelain sanitary ware, to the more obscure ones like talc and pumice (a volcanic stone used on rough skin). Even the shower screen and mirror are made from sand!

I wonder...

Water can exist in a number of states related to how hot or cold it is. It can exist as a gas in water vapour or as liquid water and as solid ice.

Presentation

If you have made decorative items made of clay or other moulded material, use these as the basis for a display. Make sure that students display their work either with an instructional text on how the material has been transformed or with captions.

Plenary

Ask students in groups to put together a short sequence of dramatic actions to illustrate a change in a material, e.g. being run over by a steam roller, or stood on by an elephant. Can the other students guess what the dramas represent and if so can they say whether the change is reversible or not?

Unit 2: Materials – Heating up

The objectives for this lesson are that students should be able to:

- Carry out practical investigations

- Make observations and describe their findings

- Describe how heating can change some materials into new and useful materials

- Discover how some materials change when they are heated

- Learn that some of these changes are reversible

- Learn that some of these changes are irreversible.

SB p.22 | *Starter*

Talk about materials that change when they are heated. *Why does chocolate melt in your hand? What happens to ice cream on a sunny day?* Elicit the answer that when heated, chocolate, butter and ice cream all melt and get softer but when clay is baked it gets harder. Look at the illustration on *Student Book* page 22. Describe what is happening. *How has each material changed?* It may soften, melt or become liquid, and in some cases change even more. *Which of these could change back again if cooled?*

SB pp.22–23 | *Explain*

Melting moments

Heat can change some materials and not others. Heat changes chocolate by melting, changing the solid chocolate into liquid chocolate. Many students mix up the concepts of melting and dissolving so use this opportunity to physically enact 'melting' with the students – just like the clocks in Dali's painting. Emphasize that by melting the chocolate we change the way it behaves (make it runny). When the chocolate cools again it will be solid as it was before.

Chocolate, butter and ice cream are all foods that melt when the temperature is warm. To stop this from happening, the only thing the students could do is to make sure the foods were cooled and kept below their melting temperature either

by bringing them indoors into a cooler area, or putting them in a fridge or a cool bag.

Other substances that students may have seen melting in the hot sun are ice, wax or tar on very hot roads.

Many foods are changed when they are cooked. Discuss different types of cooked egg, and baking cakes or bread. *Which of these changes are reversible?*

> ⚠️ Closely supervise the heating activities.
>
> Thorough hygiene is required if you plan for students to eat the foods.
>
> Check for any food allergies and diabetes.
>
> Ensure adult cooking demonstrations are in safe conditions.

Things to do | WS 18

Marvellous mixtures

Put squares of chocolate, marshmallows, and rice cereal in three separate bowls. Stand each over a pan of hot (not boiling) water. *What do you think will happen?* When the chocolate has melted, mix all three ingredients together. *What will happen now?* Put the mixture into individual cake cases, cool, and refrigerate until the chocolate has solidified. Enjoy the end results! Students can record the recipe on WS18.

Make soft cheese. Warm (to hand-hot) 100 ml of full fat milk. Then add about 20 ml of lemon juice. Watch closely when you stir the lemon into the milk and it begins to cool. *Can you see it curdle?* Strain the mixture through a clean, folded J-cloth; as the liquid passes through, solid cheese is left behind. Squeeze the cloth gently, turn out the small ball of solid cheese, sprinkle with salt and taste.

Shake up some double cream in a tightly lidded plastic jar until the liquid separates into butter (a solid) and whey (a liquid, mainly water). Can students hear a difference as they shake and the solid butter begins to form?

Explore foods further. Add warm water to dried pasta and leave it to soak. *How does the pasta change?* Do the same to couscous or semolina, rice or pulses, or porridge.

44

Using a container inside a pan of hot water, demonstrate melting wax to make candles. Pour the molten wax into candle moulds, or make sand candles where shapes have been pressed into damp sand to create a mould. Remember to insert a wick before the wax sets. Mix in grated wax crayons to add colour.

Demonstrate making toffee by melting sugar and butter. Also demonstrate honeycomb toffee: heat four dessertspoons of sugar and two dessertspoons of golden syrup to boiling point and stir in half to one teaspoon of bicarbonate of soda. The mixture will fizz and expand. It sets hard when left to cool. *Can you see the air spaces in the toffee?* Take great care as toffee reaches very high temperatures.

Can you get the milk and lemon juice back from the cheese or the milk back from the butter and whey? What would happen if you let the pasta, rice, porridge, etc. dry out again? Where does the water go? What happens to the wax when you burn candles?

With bought (or baked) bread, enjoy a class picnic with the cheese and butter, followed by the crispy cakes.

Differentiation

More able students could list things that melt and things that go hard when they are heated. With supervision, they can change plastic crisp packets with heat. Put empty packets on a baking tray in a low-heat oven; they will shrink to tablets. Drill the corner to make a key ring. *What did the heat do?*

Support less able students by reinforcing knowledge and vocabulary of the changes that happen during heating and cooling of the chocolate. Let them hold chocolate in their hand to feel the warmth melt it.

Dig deeper

Ice cream keeps its particular qualities because the cream from which it is made becomes solid as it freezes. Above freezing, the cream in the ice cream begins to melt and change state from a solid to a liquid. Other changes occur too as the air which is whipped in to the ice cream ceases to be held in the frozen mixture and escapes. For an interesting investigation try comparing the time it takes for different brands of ice cream to melt.

Did you know?

Chocolate as we know it today is a relatively recently invented food. It is a processed food made from the beans of the Cacao tree found in the tropical rainforest. Cacao beans were used by the Maya Indians hundreds of years ago. They roasted the beans, and added chilli and other spices to make a drink called Xocolati.

I wonder...

Not all chocolate melts or solidifies at the same rate or at the same temperature. The rate of melting or the temperature the chocolate melts at depends on the percentage of fats, milks and cocoa solids in the final mix.

Presentation

Make a flow chart of the processes you have used to make your crispy cakes or cheese. Use photographs of the process to enhance the display.

Plenary

Make a collection of pictures of foodstuffs that have been 'changed' in some way by melting or cooking and ask the students to spot what has changed e.g. melted cheese on a pizza, hard-boiled egg, solidified chocolate sauce on ice cream, etc. Recap on different types of changes that have been explored so far.

45

Unit 2: Materials – Disappearing acts

The objectives for this lesson are that students should be able to:

- Carry out practical investigations

- Make careful observations and record their findings

- Compare results with others

- Communicate their findings to others

- Recognize that some materials can dissolve in water

- Find out which substances dissolve and which do not.

Starter
SB p.24

Give groups of students a white plastic or ceramic plate and a handful of sweets with a hard coloured candy shell. Tell the students to arrange the sweets into a pattern on the plate and to make sure the sweets are not touching each other. Leave some space around each one. When the students are happy with their pattern, gently and slowly pour cold water onto the plate to surround but not cover the sweets. Look carefully at what happens.

The coloured sugar shell will start to dissolve and the colour 'bleeds' into the water creating attractive patterns. Explain to the students that the sweets are dissolving.

Students often confuse dissolving and melting. Remind them that melting needs heat and involves only one substance. That substances change state when heated. Dissolving doesn't need heat but does need two substances. A solute* (the substance being dissolved) and a solvent* (the liquid, usually water in schools) that the substance dissolves into.

(*students do not need to be familiar with these terms at this stage.)

The challenge
SB pp.24–25

Read the opening conversation on page 24 of the *Student Book*. Have the students ever tried anything like that? *How did the sweet disappear? What dissolved the sugar it was made from?* Refer back to the starter. The sugar in the sweet dissolved in the saliva in the mouth, saliva being mostly water, just as the candy dissolved in the water.

What to do
WS 19

Start with all of your samples (labelled) – five or six should be enough. Make sure you have a good range of substances that dissolve and don't dissolve. Include some that will change the colour of the water. Ask the students in groups to first identify each sample and predict what will happen when they mix it with water. Let the students test each substance and record their results in the table on WS19.

What you need

A collection of easily available kitchen powders and substances, e.g. salt, sugars, bicarbonate of soda, gravy powder etc. Clear plastic cups or beakers, spoons for measuring and stirring. Water in a jug.

⚠️ Take care with substances. Students should not taste their samples. Be careful not to inhale substances or get them in your eyes.

What to check

Students can double-check their results by checking with colleagues. Discuss why scientists sometimes repeat investigations lots of times.

Differentiation

There is no real need to know the names of the substances as they can just be labelled by number but more able students may enjoy the challenge of trying to work out what substances are from what they already know of their behaviours.

More able or capable students can have more samples to test and rank, taking care to be systematic in their testing. They may also choose to control for more variables such as the number of stirs or volume of water.

Students who struggle will only need to make a comparison of perhaps two or three samples.

What did you find?

Amina and Khalifa found that many of the common kitchen substances dissolved.

Is this the same with your class?

Record

Take photographs of your substances, before and after adding water.

Put a clear glass beaker on white paper. Place a coloured boiled sweet in the beaker, or a coloured sugar cube and add warm water. As the coloured sugar dissolves in the water it radiates outwards making attractive patterns. Use warm water to speed the process up.

Can you do better?

Stirring materials that can dissolve in water usually helps them to dissolve more quickly. This is why we stir tea when adding sugar. However, for this test, as long as they stir the materials to the same extent and for about the same time in each case, this will not affect the results of the investigation. Stirring is one of the variables in the investigation which has to be kept constant.

Now predict

As with stirring, using warm water will affect the speed of dissolving of many materials. Therefore in order to compare solubilities fairly, it is necessary to keep the water temperature the same throughout. The children can use warm water – and it may make many materials dissolve more quickly – but if they do, then they should use warm water with all the materials in order for the investigation to be a fair test.

Did you know?

Sweets or candy are largely sugar, with colouring and flavouring. There are thousands of different variations! Try investigating a few sugar-based sweets (not chocolates) and put them in a cup of water. Do they all eventually dissolve?

Presentation

Use the photographs you have taken of 'candy rangoli' patterns to create a colourful display showing the colouring in the candy coating dissolving in water.

Plenary

Although it looks as if a substance, for example sugar, which has dissolved in water, has disappeared, in fact it has not. The particles have been spread throughout the water so we can't see them. We know they are still there; if we taste the water, it will be sweet.

New International Edition

Unit 2: Materials – Unit 2 Review

The objectives for this lesson are that students should be able to:

- Check what they have learned about materials in this Unit

- Find out how they are working within the Grade 2 level.

SB p.26

Expectations

Students working towards Grade 2 level will:

- Describe how heating can change some materials

- Describe how to change a material's shape by bending, twisting and stretching

- Recognize a rock

- Make observations which, with help, they record in tables.

In addition, students working within Grade 2 level will:

- Identify some naturally occurring materials

- Recognize some rocks from their appearance

- Give some uses of common rocks, e.g. slate for roofs

- Describe how heating can change some materials into new and useful materials

- State the dangers of hot water or naked flames

- Describe what happens to water when it is heated and cooled

- Recognize that some materials can dissolve in water

- Make predictions of what will happen when something is heated

- Record observations in tables

- Recognize when simple comparisons are unfair.

Further to this, students working beyond Grade 2 level will also:

- Describe how changes can be reversed

- Describe what happens to some materials in water

- Recognize and start to explain when a comparison is unfair.

Check-up

Although many white powders look identical, they may behave differently when mixed with other substances. Discuss how Aisha could find out what the materials are.

- Aisha could try mixing each of the powders with water and comparing them. Flour will not dissolve in water but sugar will. Icing sugar in water colours the water white because it contains a chemical to prevent clogging.

Assessment

WS 20

Use the Unit 2 Assessment on WS20 to check students' understanding of the content of the Unit. The answers are given opposite.

Name: _____ Date: _____

WS 20 Unit 2 assessment

1 You can easily squeeze or squash these materials. True or false?

rubber _____ stone _____

wood _____ brick _____

plastic _____ wool _____

metal _____

2 Join the material to where it comes from.

leather	comes from the ground.
coal	comes from a sheep.
wool	comes from trees.
wood	comes from a cow.
glass	comes from a plant.
cotton	is made from sand.

3 Choose what happens when you warm these things. Circle the word.

① dough	melts	cooks	hardens
② chocolate	hardens	freezes	melts
③ clay	burns	hardens	melts
④ wax	cooks	melts	hardens
⑤ ice	hardens	cooks	melts

4 Write one use of granite. _____

20   Heinemann Explore Science Grade 2

Answers

1   Rubber T; wood F; plastic T; metal F; stone F; brick F; wool T.

2   Leather — comes from the ground.
    Coal — comes from a sheep.
    Wool — comes from trees.
    Wood — comes from a cow.
    Glass — comes from a plant.
    Cotton — is made from sand.

3   Dough hardens; chocolate melts; clay hardens; wax melts; ice melts.

4   Accept examples such as worktops, chopping boards, gravestones or any reasonable use of this very hard substance.

The answer!

Refer back to the original question about Mr Silly. Look at the students' ideas and drawings of Mr Silly and his things. By now the students should understand that every material will have at least one observable property and many will have several. Of all the properties that materials have, we may value one over another, e.g. glass being transparent is more important to us than it being brittle. Talk about which properties we value for which object and why – use everyday examples you would find in the classroom, home or town.

And finally...

Display natural materials alongside pictures of where they come from (such as a feather next to a picture of a duck).

Many traditional tales, stories and poems from European culture feature objects made from strange materials or used in unusual ways, e.g. Cinderella's glass slipper, Hansel and Gretel's gingerbread house or the Jumblies going to sea in a sieve (Edward Lear). Can the students think of any tales from their own culture that have a similar premise or can they invent their own story which features an object made from an unusual material, e.g. a carpet of nails or a dress of leaves?

49

Unit 3: Light and dark

The objectives for this Unit are that students should be able to:

- Identify different light sources including the Sun.

- Know that darkness is the absence of light.

- Identify shadows.

- Explore ways of changing shadows.

- Make simple measurements.

- Make suggestions for collecting evidence.

- Talk about risks and how to avoid danger.

- Make and record observations.

SB p.27   *Science background*

This section develops students' understanding of the need for light to see things. Students learn that darkness is the absence of light and that the Sun is our main source of light in the daytime. They learn to differentiate between sources of light and reflectors of light.

Work in this Unit also offers opportunities for students to relate their understanding of science to everyday experiences of light and darkness and to health and safety.

Visually impaired students will need particular support in this Unit. They will be able to take part in activities through careful use of residual vision, through their awareness that many light sources are also heat sources and through using their sense of touch. It is important for teachers to help normally sighted students to be sensitive to those who are visually impaired.

The key concepts in this Unit are that light travels from a source and that we see because light enters our eyes, that light is unable to pass through some materials causing shadows, and that surfaces reflect light.

Where does light come from?

Light is a form of energy given off by particles of matter which have been 'excited' - some energy has been given to them. Light comes from a light source. The energy is generally provided either by heating, burning or by passing electricity through a filament or a gas. Heat and light are produced by a normal light bulb and the Sun, while fluorescent lamps and advertising signs contain gas. Some modern energy-saving lights are fluorescent tubes folded into the compact space of a bulb. Some animals are able to generate light – a process known as bioluminescence.

How fast does light travel?

Light travels very fast. When we turn on a light bulb, light floods the room almost instantaneously. Light travels at 300,000 km per second (186,000 miles per second). Even at this speed, light from the Sun takes 8 minutes to reach Earth. This means that when we look at the Sun, the light entering our eye set out 8 minutes ago, so we are seeing the Sun not as it is now but as it was 8 minutes ago. We may see light from the stars that has been travelling for thousands of years before reaching our eyes.

How does light travel?

Light travels in straight lines. Look at the light from a spotlight or a bright torch beam shining through the gap in curtains or blinds. If chalk dust or talc is scattered into the beam, the straight path of the light can be clearly seen. Light from a laser is a clear example of light travelling in straight lines; lasers are now commercially available to schools as tools for measuring, or for creating straight lines in building work. Here the light can be seen travelling over very long distances in a straight line.

What are shadows?

Because light travels in straight lines we get shadows. The shadows produced on a wall by your hand, or your shadow on the yard on a sunny day, have fairly sharp edges. If light travelled in curved lines, it would bend around your body or hand so that the edge of the shadow would be more diffuse.

Shadows are caused when objects block light. We call such objects opaque. Opaque objects do not allow light to pass through them. On a sunny day you can see a shadow of yourself on the ground. Because your body is opaque, the light that hits it from behind does not reach the ground in front of you. As a result, this part of the ground appears darker to your eye than the surrounding ground, which is receiving the full sunlight. Light from the Sun has travelled such a great distance that sunlight strikes the Earth in parallel lines.

Some lights, however, do not make sharp shadows. Fluorescent lamps, which produce their light from a long glass tube, produce shadows that are very soft and lack sharp edges. Light from a large source can leak round the edges of an object, producing a deep umbra and a shadowy penumbra. For classroom work, use torches or simple desk lamps as a light source that you can control easily.

Light can also pass through some objects, and these are said to be transparent or translucent. The word 'transparent' is usually applied to materials which allows light to pass through them so that we can see objects through them. Materials which allow only a little light to pass through them, or which reflect or bend the path of the light as it goes through are described as translucent. They let light through, but not images. These concepts will be explored further on in the course.

Reflections

When light hits an object, some of the light is absorbed and some is reflected back. A mirror reflects almost all the light that strikes it. A glass mirror has a thin coating of aluminium on the back and it is this thin coating, not the glass, which reflects most of the light. Mirrors reflect an image.

Polished metal surfaces are very good reflectors, reflecting over 95 per cent of the light which hits them. Shiny but uneven surfaces reflect as much light, but in a more random, diffuse way and do not reflect images. Whether something gives a reflected image depends on how well the light is reflected from it.

'Light' is a word with many meanings in English. It can help understanding to use the word 'lamp' to describe a source of light.

Avoid using the phrase 'see-through' for transparent materials as it reinforces the misconception that seeing is an active process. Light passes easily through transparent materials.

Practical work with light frequently demands a dark or at least a shaded classroom.

> ⚠ Advise students never to look directly at the Sun.

Language

beam	an emission of light travelling in a straight line
bright	radiating or reflecting light e.g. bright sunlight
dark	having very little or no light
day	the interval of light between sunrise and sunset
candle	a long piece of wax with an embedded wick which is burned to give light
light	the energy that makes things visible; a source of illumination e.g. the Sun
night	the hours of darkness between sunset and sunrise
opaque	the property of a material which blocks light
reflect	to bounce light back from a surface
shiny	bright or glossy in appearance; reflector of light
see	to have the power of sight; to receive and interpret light
source	the origin of something; the place from which something comes
Sun	the star at the centre of our solar system, our source of light in the day
torch	flashlight; a light to be carried in the hand, often powered by batteries
transparent	a property of a material which lets light pass through it unaltered

The key words to learn are given in the Words to learn list on page 27 of the *Student Book*.

Resources

- *Light and Dark* Reader
- Torches
- Candles or lanterns
- Strong light source for experimental use such as an overhead projector light or bright desk lamp
- Pictures of light sources including the Sun
- Pictures of objects that reflect light, e.g. the Moon, 'cat's eyes' reflecting devices in the road

New International Edition

- Selection of objects that are opaque and will cast shadows contrasting with selection of transparent objects

- Mirrors

- Shiny objects and materials that are good reflectors of light, e.g. aluminium foil, mirror card, tinsel, coloured sequins or glass baubles

- Large piece of blackout material to make a 'dark den'

- Black boxes – cardboard boxes painted black inside

- Black and white card and paper, craft materials

- Measuring tapes

Bright ideas

Thinking about light and dark can inspire many creative activities. Collecting materials which reflect light can lead to a fun and interactive display. Create a 'dark den' using heavy material draped over a table which blocks out all light and under which students can experiment with torches.

Other classroom investigations you might like to try could include:

- Which is the best reflective material?

- Which materials let light through?

- Which torch is the brightest?

- Which torch gives out the brightest light?

- How much light do we need to be able to see?

- What's the difference between being in the shade and in the Sun?

- When is the warmest part of the day?

> ⚠ Although candles are an important source of light, students should not be encouraged to play with fire.

Knowledge check

- Students will be able to indicate and name common sources of light around them. They are able to compare two different sources of light and describe the differences and similarities, such as brightness or colour. Students can make general statements about when a light gets dimmer or brighter.

- Students can recognize when shadows are formed and when light reflects. They can describe the formation of shadow or reflection. They relate the characteristics of a shadow to the object and both the position of the light and its strength.

- Students know light travels in straight lines.

Skills check

Students need to:

- use observation and communication skills.

- predict outcomes and turn ideas into a form that can be tested.

- carry out fair tests.

- be able to make simple measurements and to record their findings in simple tables or with words and pictures.

- use expressions linking cause and effect such as 'because'.

- make simple measurements of length and size.

- make simple comparisons and enter their observations and measurements in tables.

- explain the patterns they notice in their results with help.

- be able to make simple predications about what will happen in an investigation and be able to offer a reason for their prediction.

- be able to measure changes in shadows and lights and draw a simple chart.

Links to other subjects

As work on light includes items found around us every day, there are good cross-subject links including:

Literacy: Investigate stories, legends and poems that are set at night-time, particularly stories about ghosts if appropriate.

Make simple lists and write simple instructions.

Distinguish everyday from scientific language.

Describe similarities and differences.

Write labels, annotate diagrams.

Read myths and legends about the Sun, Moon and stars.

Numeracy: Use simple measures of length to measure shadows.

Investigate reflections and use mirrors to investigate symmetry.

Interpret simple graphs showing hours of daylight over the course of a month or year.

Other subjects: The science work on light and dark links to a number of other subjects:

ICT links can be made by searching the Internet or using CD-ROMs. If you have data loggers in schools, these can measure the intensity of light sources.

Art and Design – Study how light or shadow is represented in great paintings.

Use contrasting shiny and dull paper/fabric strips to weave a mat.

Make collages using shiny papers and materials using cellophane, foils, sequins, buttons, tinsel and lametta.

For beaded sewing or sticking use Indian mirror-work as a stimulus.

Create a mixture of sewing and collage using sequins, gold and silver thread, shiny fabrics. Sew on to dull fabric for contrast.

Shiny mobiles: make star or Sun shapes of foil and hang from tinsel-covered hoops. (One side of stars could carry vocabulary.)

Let's find out...

The Unit opens with this question:

Aditi has lost her pet cat. It's dark outside. The cat is black. How can she find it?

This question highlights two key areas of knowledge in Grade 2 when considering light and dark. Firstly, that the night is never truly dark; there will always be some light from the stars and if we can see the Moon it will be reflecting light from the Sun. Also, there is often light from streetlights or lights from houses. Secondly, that there is a difference between a light source, such as a torch, and a reflector of light, such as the cat collar. Students sometimes confuse light from a source with reflected light and this question can be used to draw comparisons between the two.

53

Unit 3: Light and dark – Source of light

The objectives for this lesson are that students should be able to:

• Know that light comes from a source

• Name some common light sources including the Sun

• Describe and compare light sources and discover that some light sources are brighter than others

• Recognize that shiny objects reflect light.

SB p.28 — Starter

Start with a game of charades to represent different sources of light, e.g. match, bonfire, firework, flashlight, Sun etc. Support students by giving them a picture of the light source they have to mime. *How many more can you think of?*

We take light for granted; it's all around us whenever we want it. What sources of light can students name?

Examine a range of pictures of sources of light and objects that reflect light. Can the students sort them accurately into light sources and light reflectors?

SB pp.28–29 — Explain — WS 21

Seeing in the dark

This is an introduction to the difference between a light source, something which creates light energy, and a reflector, something that reflects light. Both may appear to have light coming from them but only sources can create their own light. Activities in this Unit taken together are to enable students to know the difference between the two and to recognize that only when a light shines upon them will a reflector be seen in the dark. Note, we can see the Moon because even at night it is reflecting light from the hidden Sun.

What is a light source?

From the beginning it is important to distinguish what is a source of light from other objects which only reflect light – the most common misconceptions being that the Moon is a light source (it is not, it reflects light from the Sun) and that shiny objects, particularly mirrored objects, are light sources (they are not sources of light, they only reflect light). For example, the eyes of cats and other nocturnal animals reflect light – so the light passes through the cat's retina twice.

Showing pictures of the Moon's craters which cast shadows may help to explain this particular misconception – if the Moon was a source of light and making its own light (remember it is not) then why are there shadows on it? There are no shadows on a lit light bulb. Similarly, students may never have experienced complete darkness so try to create a really 'dark den' where they can take, for example, a plastic mirror and show that it does not generate its own light.

Make sure the students are comfortable with the concepts of making light and reflecting light. Use WS21 to help students to identify light sources. Create two lists of vocabulary labelled 'sources' and 'reflectors' and add to these as the topic progresses.

> ⚠ Emphasize to students that not all light sources are the same. Some are much brighter than others. One very bright source of light is our Sun and looking directly at the Sun should be avoided. It is such a strong source of heat and light that it can damage our eyes.

Things to do

Shiny, shiny

Show students a tin can, and ask them if they can see their reflection it. Some metal drinks cans can appear dull rather than shiny as they have a matt surface where the rays of light hitting the surface bounce off in many directions. (You can use an abrasive pad such as 'Scotchbrite' to smooth and polish the surface to a mirror finish.) Students

54

can then compare how well the can reflects light depending on how shiny it is.

Make a 'dark den' by draping a piece of blackout fabric over a table. Allow students to sit or crawl underneath to experience darkness. Make a collection of shiny or reflective objects and put them in the den. How well can students see them? Turn on a torch in your den – how well can students see the shiny objects now? Always emphasize the difference between a light source and a reflector.

Collect together examples of shiny and reflective art and craft materials and make a shiny collage or mobile.

Differentiation

More able students could research materials specifically designed to keep out light, e.g. blackout blinds used to keep rooms dark or materials used in parasols, beach umbrellas or awnings.

Less able students should be given lots of opportunities to handle and observe light sources and reflectors. Students may suggest that a shiny object will shine brightly in a dark cupboard, indicating they think it is a light source. Use your collection of shiny objects and suggest the students look at them in normal classroom light, in a black box or dark den, and when the light from a torch is shone on them. Give the students time to explore and to compare what they see in the different circumstances. Ask students what they would see if they took a black and white cat into a dark cupboard. *What would the cat see?*

Dig deeper

Celebrations using lights are widespread throughout the world and students could investigate festivals from other cultures. For example, the Swedish festival of St Lucia (the Christian patron saint of light) takes place on the 13th December, one of the longest and darkest nights of the year in Sweden. Hanukkah, or the Festival of Lights, is an 8-day Jewish holiday commemorating the rededication of the Holy Temple in Jerusalem; Diwali or Deepawali, also known as the 'festival of lights', is an important festival in Hinduism, Jainism and Sikhism.

Did you know?

Humans cannot see without light and so fire, oil, gas and electric lighting have all been important throughout history. Some animals living in very dark places have adapted to produce light by bioluminescence. Glow worms are bioluminescent insects. There are even luminous species of fungi.

I wonder...

A light on the front of a bicycle is an active device to illuminate the pathway ahead so the rider can see where they are going. The rider does not need to see where they have been so you may have reflectors rather than lights on the back of a bicycle. When another vehicle shines its headlights forward, the light will bounce off the reflector and show that there is something ahead.

Other ideas

Investigate dark places such as deep under the ocean where light cannot penetrate. Make a display of the unusual creatures that can be found there using luminous paint (obtained from educational suppliers).

Make a picture book for younger children to enjoy showing collections of light sources either drawn or cut from magazines and catalogues.

Presentation

Display as many photographs and pictures of light sources as you can in a frieze around your classroom.

Plenary

Together or in groups set your own words to the tune of a familiar nursery rhyme to summarize the differences between light sources and reflectors.

Unit 3: Light and dark – Our Sun

The objectives for this lesson are that students should be able to:

- Name the Sun as a source of light

- Learn that the Sun is our main source of light in the daytime

- Describe differences between day and night

- Learn that the Sun is a source of heat

- Understand that looking at the Sun can harm our eyes

- Be able to name and explain measures we can take to avoid being damaged by the Sun.

SB p.30 — Starter

Find a video clip or download a film clip from the Internet which shows the Sun close up. Point out the fiery solar flares that are emitted from the Sun's hot surface. The Sun is made mostly of hydrogen gas and helium gas and is by far the largest thing in our solar system.

SB pp.30–31 — Explain

Explain that the Sun is an enormous spherical ball of gas. The Earth would fit a million times in the same space. The Sun produces huge amounts of energy by combining hydrogen nuclei into helium by nuclear fusion. This is what generates so much heat and light. The Sun is the nearest star to our planet. Without the heat and light the Sun provides, the Earth would be cold, dark and without life.

Even when we cannot see it, the Sun is always there. We will explain how day and night occur later.

Ask students to think about the differences between night and day. They can use the pictures in the *Student Book* to help them.

During the day the Sun provides enough light for us to see things easily when we are out of doors. At night when the Sun is not visible, it is more difficult to see things so we use other sources of light to see.

The Sun's light is so bright in the day that other light sources may be difficult to see; for example, fireworks light up the dark night sky but in the daytime they have very little effect and are difficult to see. The stars are still in the sky by day, but the Sun's light makes them impossible to see. The Moon is there, too; and occasionally, it is visible in the daytime.

People wearing sunglasses

In very sunny places humans often wear sunglasses to protect their eyes from the brightness of the sunlight. Emphasize that students should never look directly at the Sun, even if they are wearing sunglasses, as the Sun could damage their eyes. Sunglasses only make it easier for us to see in bright light; they do not offer us protection from the Sun's rays. Viewers of eclipses of the Sun, when the Moon passes between the Sun and the Earth giving a dark 'zone of totality' in some areas, use specially made filters.

Things to do — WS 22

Sunny days

Discuss the beach scene. Ask the students about their experiences of being out of doors on very hot and sunny days. As well as providing light, the Sun also provides heat. Think about the sensation of feeling the warm Sun on your skin. Too much time in the Sun can damage skin. Look at the picture again; what can the students see that helps protect us from the damaging effects of too much sun? Ask students to complete WS22. Talk about the risks and how to avoid the danger of strong sunlight.

Differentiation

Able students may make the link between heat and light by drawing on experiences of being close to a fire or feeling the warmth of a light bulb. Emphasize this link with less able students by taking the class outside on a sunny day and physically moving between light and shade. What do they notice? As well as appearing darker, the shaded areas will be cooler as the Sun's heat as well as its light is blocked. Architects and garden designers in very sunny countries frequently incorporate shaded areas in their designs to give relief from the heat of the Sun.

Dig deeper

Animals such as geckos and lizards are 'cold-blooded' reptiles that need the heat from the Sun to maintain their body heat. Mammals and birds can regulate their temperature and maintain their body heat even when the temperature is low. We are 'warm-blooded' because we maintain a stable body temperature. Cold-blooded creatures are at the temperature of their surroundings. They cool down at night and bask in the Sun to raise their body temperature for activity. Cold-blooded animals do not have to use a lot of food energy to maintain a constant temperature like mammals. They can survive when temperatures are low and food is scarce.

Did you know?

The Sun's surface temperature is around 5,500° Celsius and fifteen million degrees Celsius at the core. Compare that to your average domestic oven, reaching around 220°C!

I wonder…

The Sun is a star. Every star in the night sky is a sun and we are beginning to discover that other suns have planets like ours orbiting them. It is only in the last 100 years that astronomers have begun to understand what a star is made from and they have classified them into different types. Our Sun is a yellow G-type star. The hottest, brightest stars are called Blue Giants.

Other ideas

WS 23

Because of the Sun's huge influence on Earth, many early cultures saw the Sun as a god or deity to be worshipped. For example, Ancient Egyptians had a Sun god called Ra, while in Aztec mythology there is a Sun god named Tonatiuh. Find stories of Sun gods and Moon gods from other cultures.

Make a poster on WS23, warning about the dangers of staying too long in the Sun and encouraging people to use protective sun creams or to stay in the shade. Too much sunlight can make us dehydrated – find out how much water we should be drinking to stay healthy in hot weather. Again discuss the risks and danger of long exposure to sunlight.

Presentation

On your discovery table, display resources and artefacts associated with sun protection, e.g. different types of sunglasses, sun creams, sun hats, parasols etc.

Plenary

Use the posters the students have created to reinforce messages of staying safe in the sun. Talk about keeping cool and hydrated as well as protecting skin and eyes from harsh sunlight.

Unit 3: Light and dark – Using light

The objectives for this lesson are that students should be able to:

- Know that we need light to see

- Learn that darkness is the absence of light

- Explain how we use light to help us when it is dark and give examples of this.

SB p.32 | *Starter*

Transform your classroom into a dark place. Cover over the windows with black paper or card, draw curtains or close blinds if you have them, switch off all the lights. *How does the classroom feel different? Is it easy to see things or not?*

Cover your eyes with a sleep mask or blindfold and try to identify everyday objects using your other senses. Emphasize that we cannot see when there is no light at all and how important light is to us.

List all the ways in which we use light, e.g. to help us light up rooms when it is night time, to signal warning, to give messages, traffic lights for example.

SB pp.32–33 | *Explain* | WS 24

Artificial light

The Sun is our major source of natural light. Some creatures can produce their own light to help them find food or to attract other creatures. Humans can't create light with their bodies but we have created technologies to make light for us. Many of these lights are powered by electricity from the mains or batteries. Discuss the fact that different light sources produce different levels of brightness. Students can complete WS24, which offers an opportunity for simple, practical comparisons.

Discuss with the students other ways that we use lights. Many religions use lights or candles as part of a ceremony; for example candles are used in ritual Buddhist observances and there are candle festivals in Thailand.

Think about lights to signal danger such as warning lights on dangerous roads or railways, or the light from a lighthouse to warn about undersea rocks or shallows.

When we are driving a car at night we switch on headlights to see and inside the car the dashboard instruments are illuminated. Pilots in a plane at night have runway lights to guide them.

Things to do

The black box

Use a black box to investigate light. Any box will do but ordinary shoe boxes with a lid are just about the right size for small children to handle with ease. The aim is to create an enclosed space students can see into but where no light can get in, creating a totally dark space inside the box. Cover the inside of the box with black paper or paint the inside black so that any light entering cannot be reflected back. Cut a small peep hole in one end of the box and look inside. The box should be totally black and dark. Objects placed in the black box cannot be seen unless light enters. Either open the lid or cut a second hole in the box that can be covered over or opened at will. Reinforce the idea that without light we cannot see.

Differentiation

More able students might like to investigate how we see different colours. We see colour because white light (normal daylight) is made up of a mixture of colours. They can investigate how colours appear to change when viewed through different colours of acetates.

Less able students can investigate how the colour of light can be changed by covering torches in coloured acetates to make red or green lights. *How might we use this to act as a signal?*

Dig deeper

Warning beacons or fires were once used to signal danger or invasion. On a dark night, these lights could be seen for many miles. The first mapping of India by Everest, the man who gave his name to the mountain, was largely achieved at night using beacons that were lit on hills and mountains.

Today we use light to send messages through fibre optic cables made of silica to transmit telephone signals, Internet communications, and cable television signals. Students can research the work of Indian scientist Kumar Patel who pioneered the use of lasers.

58

Students can invent their own code or use Morse code but use flashes of torch light to signal messages to others.

Did you know?

Bioluminescence is common in deep-sea fish, and you can see it today in some nocturnal insects like glow-worms and fireflies. The light is produced by the oxidation of a chemical called luciferin. It is made without heat. The light is used for communication, camouflage, or luring prey. Look at animals like the angler fish, deep-sea jellyfish and other marine creatures as well as some species of centipedes and millipedes that are bioluminescent.

I wonder...

Although we may think that it is dark at night, it is never truly dark on the surface of the Earth. There is often sunlight reflected from the Moon and light from stars. Many cities have street lighting which gives off a glow even several miles away. It is only in deep caves underground and at the bottom of the deep oceans that light cannot penetrate at all and it can be said to be truly dark.

Other ideas

Create artworks using only light and dark. Use charcoal on white paper or white chalk on black paper.

Investigate what clothing we can wear to make us more visible in darkness. *Which colours show up the clearest in the dark?*

Find stories or poems that are set in the night-time. Write a contrast poem that explores the differences between dark and light. Read or invent stories about shadow people or shadows that come to life!

Presentation

Display contrasting pictures of photographs of landmarks in your area, one set taken during the day and the other at night. Able students may be able to translate the features and differences into a Venn diagram showing what is different in both pictures and what features they share. Display their work alongside the photographs.

Plenary

Think about situations where students would find themselves in a dark place. Make up a class short story or poem (written together or spoken) based upon the idea of, 'When the lights went out', where lights feature as warnings, signals and signposts.

Ask students to imagine a world with no natural light. *What would people who lived in this dark world look like? What would they eat?*

Unit 3: Light and dark – Shady shadows

The objectives for this lesson are that students should be able to:

- Understand that darkness is the absence of light
- Discover that some materials block light
- Learn how we get shadows when light is blocked
- Describe and compare the features of shadows.

SB p.34 | **Starter**

Shine a very bright light onto a screen or wall in a darkened room. With the light behind you, cast hand shadows onto the wall. *Can you make your hands into the shadow shape of a bird or an animal?* Let the students experiment making different shapes. Point out that their hands need to be between the light source and the cast shadow.

SB pp.34–35 | **Explain** | **WS 25**

Making a shadow

Light travels in straight lines. Look at the light from a spotlight or a bright torch or a beam of light shining through the gap in curtains or blinds. If chalk dust or talc is scattered into the beam, the straight path of the light can be seen.

All objects are not the same. Some are made of transparent material, like glass, which lets light pass through almost unchanged, but others block light and do not let light pass through them. We say these objects are opaque. Opaque objects cast strong shadows.

Some students may need encouragement to look closely and observe shadows. They may draw shadows with details such as patterns on them. Their human shadows may have eyes and a nose drawn on them. All shadows are without detail.

Shadows resemble the shape of the object that made them, although they may at times appear elongated or distorted depending on the angle of the light hitting the object.

What made these shadows?

Allow students to explore the shapes of shadows they create using different objects. Ask them to complete WS25 to identify objects from their shadows.

Research the art of the silhouette or outline portrait profiles popularly cut out of black card. Students can stand between a light source and paper on a wall. As they cast a shadow of their head in profile onto the paper, another student can carefully draw around the shadow outline. Cut out all of the silhouettes and make a class display. *Can we identify people from their silhouette?*

Things to do

Make a shadow

Humans are opaque. Light does not pass through us and we cast shadows with our bodies. One of the most active and engaging ways of investigating shadows is to take the students out on a yard on a sunny day and make as many different shadow shapes with their bodies as they can. Challenge them to make big shadows, small shadows, spiky or rounded shadow shapes. Get them to work individually, and in pairs and groups. Take digital photographs of each child's favourite shadow shape to incorporate in a display.

Draw attention to shadows having no details; you cannot see your face or school uniform in a shadow, only the shape you make. Also, notice that you are joined to your shadow. There is no gap between where your feet end and where your shadow starts. Some things are disconnected from their shadows on the ground. Can the students guess what they might be? Clouds, planes, birds and other flying objects cast shadows without being directly connected to them.

Indoor shadows

A similar exploration can take place indoors if outdoors is not a suitable environment. Try to find a strong light source and a large space for students to use and explore. Tell students not to look directly into the light.

Differentiation

More able students could investigate whether they can make shadows from non-opaque materials. Can they investigate changing the colour of a shadow? *Is this possible?*

Less able students should work with support to securely recognize the main features of shadows, e.g. attached to the object that makes the shadow, no detail, uniform colour, same shape as object etc. They should be given more opportunities to investigate and reinforce learning.

Dig deeper

Shadow puppetry began thousands of years ago in China and India. In Indonesia, shadow plays are an integral part of traditional culture.

Traditional shadow puppets are flat and made of leather with punched holes to suggest facial features or clothing. The separate pieces of the puppet are joined together with wire. Students can make shadow puppets out of any material you have so long as it casts a shadow – you could even cut out holes in the puppet and cover the holes with colourful cellophane – what might that shadow look like?

I wonder...

While outdoors, play a game of trying to jump on the head of your own shadow. *Is it possible?*

Other ideas

A type of photosensitive paper called 'Sun Print' paper is available through educational suppliers or via the Internet. When opaque objects are placed on the paper and the paper is exposed to sunlight, the light is blocked. The exposed paper changes colour in the sunlight and the resulting image of the object can be fixed on the paper by dipping in water. Students can investigate which objects, for example flowers, leaves or even domestic objects, give the best results.

Presentation

Use your silhouettes of students to make a display around the classroom. Link the silhouettes to photographs of profile portraits of the same students.

Plenary

Make silhouettes of staff members or of animals – can the students guess who is who just by looking at the shadow images?

Unit 3: Light and dark – Exploring shadows

The objectives for this lesson are that students should be able to:

- Plan an investigation
- Engage in practical investigations
- Make predictions
- Compare results
- Discover what makes a shadow
- Find out which material makes the best shadow.

SB p.36   Starter

These activities and explorations are built around students producing a shadow puppet show. They could use time in their literacy lessons to plan and write their play script. As an introduction, show students a real shadow puppet, one you have made or a picture of one and explain how they work. Ask students to choose a story they would like to produce as a shadow puppet play.

The challenge

Read the opening conversation on page 36 of the *Student Book*. By now the students should know quite a lot about how shadows are made but this can be an opportunity for further investigations using different materials to cast shadows.

What to do

Start with all of your material samples (labelled) – eight or ten should be enough. Make sure you have a good range of materials represented, including opaque, transparent and translucent. Ask the students in groups to first identify each material and predict what will happen when they try to use it to cast a shadow. Let the students test each material and record their results in a table of their own design. Notice that even transparent materials (plastic, cellophane, bubble wrap) cast a pale shadow.

What you need

A collection of easily available domestic materials, objects and fabrics, e.g. cotton, felt, paper, card, foil, cellophane, bubble wrap, plastic, sequins, lolly sticks and so on; a strong light source such as an overhead projector light or strong torch.

⚠️ Take care with bright lights; as with the Sun, students should avoid looking directly into the light.

What to check

Make sure the students understand that they are testing and changing only the material they will make the puppets from. Everything else – the distance they hold the material from the light, the size and the shape of the material – they should keep the same. Students can double-check their results with colleagues. Discuss why scientists sometimes repeat investigations lots of times.

Differentiation

More able or capable students can have more samples to test and rank them, taking care to be systematic in their testing. They may choose to investigate further and list the 'darkness' of different shadows in a shadow scale.

Students who struggle will only need to make a comparison of perhaps two or three samples.

What did you find?   WS 26

Noor and Saad found that all of the darkest shadows were made by opaque materials – materials that they could not see through. However, some of the transparent materials did make some shadows but very pale ones and generally around the edges of the shapes they had cut out. Ask the students to identify the materials that they found made good shadows on WS26.

Is this the same with your class?

Can you do better?

The children should have no difficulty in placing the opaque materials into the group of materials that make good shadows. But useful discussion may arise with translucent or transparent materials which allow some light through, but still cast some kind of shadow. Curved transparent objects, such as water bottles or even glass lenses, cause light to be deviated; so although they do let light through, it doesn't fall where it would if the bottle or lens was not there, so it does cause a shadow of sorts. Discuss with the children whether this constitutes a shadow to not. This will help them to develop a more precise definition of the word 'shadow'.

Now predict

Ask the students what they think about Saad's prediction on page 37 of the *Student Book*. This raises the same issues about deviated light causing a shadow.

Presentation

Use photographs and captions to make a display board showing the step-by-step process of carrying out your fair test. Emphasize the variable that was measured and that only one variable was changed. You might also display your results table and the objects you used in your test.

Students could make up and present simple shadow puppet plays to the class.

Plenary

Vote on the best material to make your puppets with and allow students to design and make their own.

New International Edition

Unit 3: Light and dark – Changing shadows

The objectives for this lesson are that students should be able to:

- Learn that light travels in straight lines

- Know that when light is blocked a shadow is made

- Discover that shadows can be changed

- Explore by investigation ways to change shadows.

SB pp.38–39 | **Starter**

Pre-prepare some photographs which are spoiled either by the Sun being too much in focus and everything else being dark or by shadows being cast over the subject of the photograph.

Ask the students to imagine they are a photographer at an important event. Where do they need to stand in relation to the Sun: with the Sun in front or behind them? How can they avoid shadows being cast over the subject of their photograph? Let the students investigate using digital cameras if possible for a quick result.

What do the students think makes a technically good photograph, i.e. one where the subject is well enough lit to see features but not so well lit as to be obscured?

SB pp.38–39 | **Explain** | **WS 27**

In straight lines

We know that light travels from a light source in straight lines. It does not bend around objects. If an opaque object is in the path of light then a shadow will be formed. Try using a light box or your black box to show straight beams of light. Look at a comb and torch. Can students offer the beginnings of an explanation for what happens (light travels in straight lines through the spaces between the teeth of the comb but the teeth of the comb themselves are made of an opaque material which blocks the light)?

Making a change

In this concept cartoon the children are trying to decide if shadows are always the same or can be changed. Students know already that shadows can

be the same shape as the object that blocked the light to make them and they have investigated the kinds of materials that make the best shadows. Now they need to investigate how to change the shadows they have made.

Shadows could be made bigger by making the puppet bigger; however, there is another way as Saad suggests.

Discuss with the students their ideas on this and ask students to complete WS27.

Things to do

Getting bigger

Set up the equipment as you did in the silhouette activity with a strong light source shining on a wall. Now use the puppets the students have made to investigate how the shadows change. Ask them to place their puppet at measured intervals from the wall to the light source. At each interval (10 cm or 20 cm each time) draw around the shadow of the puppet (it is best to keep the puppet very simple for this activity – just a simple circle or square shape will be enough). Mark the distance on each outline. What is the relationship between distance from the wall and size of shadow?

Differentiation

Very able students may be able to map the changes in size of the puppet's shadow as it moves closer to the source of light, but most will be able to recognize the link between the distance from the light source and size of the shadow. That is, if an object is further away from the light source, the shadow of the object gets smaller. If an object is near to the light source, the shadow of that object is larger.

Dig deeper

A lunar eclipse is a very special event where the Earth (like the puppet) in its orbit is between the Sun (the source of light) and the Moon. The Earth casts its shadow on the Moon.

I wonder…

Shadows happen in an absence of light so they are always dark. They can however vary in tone, depending on how opaque or transparent an object is. An umbra, caused by an absence of light, is not coloured. But a penumbra may be coloured; shadows on snow may be blue in colour.

64

Shining a light through cellophane or coloured glass in ornamental windows does not cast a shadow but does change the colour of the light we see.

Other ideas

The shapes of a shadow change in relation to the position of the light source. Encourage the students to investigate this using a simple opaque object such as book or a cup. Ask them to investigate how to change the shape of the shadow by changing the position of the light source. Moving the light source further from the object will make the shadow smaller but what about the angle the light is hitting the object? How will that change the shape of the shadow?

Investigate how shadows change throughout the day as the position of the light source (the Sun) changes. Students should notice that in the morning and evening shadows get longer and are in opposite directions, whilst at midday, when the sun is at its highest, shadows are small. They can then complete WS28.

Presentation

Students have been working on puppet plays. Present their work to the whole school or year group in an assembly or to parents (make sure to add a small section to explain the science of how shadows are made) or present to another class or group of younger students.

Plenary

Students will have been working on the theme of 'shadow puppets'. If they have made their own puppets, allow them to act out a short scene from their puppet play. Alternatively you can download a scene from a shadow puppet play from the Internet to view and talk abut how the shadows are made, how the shadows could be changed and where the light source needs to be in order to cast a shadow of the puppet.

Unit 3: Light and dark – Unit 3 Review

The objectives for this lesson are that students should be able to:

- Check what they have learned about light and dark in this Unit

- Find out how they are working within the Grade 2 level.

SB p.40 **Expectations**

Students working towards Grade 2 level will:

- Name a number of light sources including the Sun

- Recognize that they cannot see in complete darkness

- Know that it is dangerous to look at the Sun.

In addition, students working within Grade 2 level will:

- Describe and make comparisons of a number of light sources

- Explain why it is dangerous to look at the Sun

- Recognize and identify a shadow

- Make simple measurements.

Further to this, students working beyond Grade 2 level will also:

- Explain that they cannot see shiny objects in the dark because they are not light sources

- Make simple comparisons about shadows.

Check-up

Discuss the mistakes in Arundahti's picture, which shows common misconceptions that young children hold about shadows.

- Shadows are usually joined to the object that makes them, the exceptions being floating or flying objects such as clouds, birds, balloons etc.

- Shadows do not have detail and generally are the shape of the object that casts them.

Assessment WS 29 WS 30

Use the Unit 3 Assessment on WS29 and WS30 to check students' understanding of the content of the Unit. The answers are given opposite.

Name: _____ Date: _____

WS 29 Unit 3 assessment 1

1 Tick three light sources.

candle   owl's eyes   torch

light bulb   mirror   window

2 We see the Sun in the daytime and the Moon at night. Which is a light source? Tick the light source.

Unit 3: Light and dark   29

Name: _____ Date: _____

WS 30 Unit 3 assessment 2

3 Tick the right answer.
 The Sun's light can hurt your eyes because:
 a) it is so bright ☐
 b) it shines all day ☐
 c) it is a light source ☐

4 Hassan was exploring the cave. What could he take to help him to see?

5 Why is that the best thing to take?

6 Draw where Safia's shadow will be on the picture.

30   Heinemann Explore Science Grade 2

Answers

1   Candle, torch and light bulb ticked

2   Sun ticked.

3   **a)** because it is so bright.

4   Accept answers appropriate to the level of the students. Any portable light source such as a torch or lantern.

5   Accept answers appropriate to the level of the students. They might describe safety, portability, size, or brightness etc.

6   Safia's shadow should be long and to the right, reflect Safia's shape and be joined to her feet.

The answer!

Refer back to the original question about Aditi's lost cat. This question is designed to show that reflectors, like the reflective material on the collar of the cat, are not sources of light in themselves and so require another light to reflect off them. Aditi would not be able to see the reflecting collar without a light being shone upon it.

And finally...

Light and reflected light can be very beautiful. Collect a selection of coloured glass or acetates and cellophanes and make 'stained glass windows' or 'sun catchers'. Hang cut glass or crystal shapes or prisms in a sunny window to create rainbow lights. Make or use kaleidoscopes with mirrors and shiny sequins.

New International Edition

Unit 4: Electricity

The objectives for this Unit are that students should be able to:

- Distinguish between common appliances that use mains and battery electricity.

- Recognize the components of simple circuits involving cells (batteries).

- Explain why some circuits work and others do not.

- Know how a switch can be used to break a circuit.

- Describe the dangers associated with mains electricity.

- Talk about risks and how to avoid danger.

- Talk about predictions, the outcome and why this happened.

SB
p.41   *Science background*

This Unit introduces students to electricity in everyday life, electrical safety and making simple working circuits.

Students will discover how electricity is used in a variety of ways and have opportunities to engage in practical activities creating a range of electrical circuits including those incorporating switches. They will also be introduced to scientific language relating to electricity and circuits and learn how to draw electrical circuits in pictures.

Electricity is secondary energy. You can't mine electricity, grow it or pick it from a tree. It is generated by movement or by the chemicals in a battery or cell (cell is the singular form; more than one linked cell is referred to as a battery). It is convenient because it can be portable and can be used wherever you can put a battery or a wire. Small batteries push safe, low-voltage electricity round a circuit; huge generators push lethal, high-voltage electricity through transformers to our communities.

It is a common misconception that batteries are somehow full of electricity and that connecting them up in the circuit uses up all this electricity, and then the battery is empty (or 'flat'). But that's not how it is.

Electricity is a flow of minute particles called electrons, which bump each other like train trucks.

These electrons are all in the circuit to begin with, but the battery provides the 'push' that sets them on their way, travelling around the circuit and doing some work on the way.

Electrical conductors and insulators

Electricity can only flow around a circuit if materials that are good electrical conductors are used. Good electrical conductors are metals, but the carbon in pencil 'lead' is a good conductor too.

Other materials such as paper, wood, fabric and plastic are not very good conductors and we call these electrical insulators.

Thick wires allow current to flow through more easily than thin wires, just like water through a wide pipe. The flow of electricity through the thin wire filament in a light bulb heats it up and makes it glow white.

Circuits

The components in the circuit affect the way the electricity flows. But wherever the electricity is measured, the result will always be the same – there are no weak or strong points. The same amount of electricity flows through every part.

Most students have difficulty with the idea of electricity flowing all the way around a circuit and back to the battery. This difficulty is reinforced by their observations that 'one wire' leads to most electrical devices. This makes them think of electricity as flowing from a source to a consumer – where electricity is used up.

Electrical energy can be converted to light and heat, to sound or to movement; it can light a bulb, make a buzzer work or a bell ring, or make a motor go around. For electricity to work in a circuit, the circuit must be complete.

Often we use switches to deliberately put a break in the circuit in order to control the flow of electricity in a circuit. When the circuit is complete and unbroken, the electricity flows through it and the component, such as a buzzer, bell or in a domestic setting the light or microwave oven, works. The switch is closed and the electricity flows. When the switch is open, this creates a break in the circuit and the electricity cannot flow across the gap, so the component does not work.

Only very high voltages of electricity can travel through the air, so a gap in a circuit stops the flow of electricity. Switches simply allow a gap in the circuit and this gap can be opened and closed, breaking or completing the circuit. The switch can be sited anywhere in the circuit and doesn't have to come 'after' the battery or 'before' the component. The simplest circuit is a 'series circuit' where the bulbs or components are in a single loop.

When students are working on circuits, stop them every now and again to ask questions. Their answers will show how much they understand. You may have to give them some prompts to help them sort out their problems. Praise and encourage students at every opportunity. Don't hurry them to complete all the challenges – work can be carried over from one session to another.

Circuits can be recorded and shown using either pictures or standard symbols. However, conventional symbols are not essential in Grades 1 and 2, and students can just draw simple pictures of the components.

Batteries

A battery contains chemicals which, when the circuit is complete, provide the 'push' to make electricity move around the circuit. Batteries have their voltage recorded on the side, for example 4.5V or 1.5V. These voltages should be matched to the bulb being used. If the battery is too large for the bulb (a 4.5V battery with a 1.5V bulb) then the bulb will blow. If a 1.5V battery is used with a 4.5V bulb then the bulb will not be very bright. We use a battery in the classroom to make components such as bulbs and buzzers work for safety reasons. Do not use rechargeable batteries for classroom circuit work as, when freshly charged, they can produce a voltage far greater than their labelling, heating up thin wires, and then can overheat themselves and components.

On a battery, you will notice that the two terminals are marked '+' and '–'. The flow is from the negative to the positive, and if more than one battery needs to work together, the terminals must all face the same way and push in the same direction. Place them + to – and then + to – again. (The only time you should connect + to + and – to – is when you jump-start a car.)

Making connections

When young students are asked to light a bulb, they know that the battery is important. But they seldom know how to make the connections from battery to bulb. They mostly think that one

wire is needed to carry electricity from battery to bulb. Even older students who know that two wires are involved may be confused about their purpose. They may think that the currents 'clash' – coming at the bulb from both directions – or are 'consumed'. Explain that the wires, for example to a television and lamp, are double – the electricity flows to the device and back again. Show a piece of unconnected two-strand wire to prove the point.

Even if students appreciate the idea of electricity flowing around the circuit, they may think that different things will happen 'upstream' and 'downstream' from a bulb.

Give students several analogies to help them visualize the flow of electricity: water through pipes, runners in a race, a train on a track, a bicycle chain. Research has shown that students offered just one analogy were no better off than students without a model. Several models are needed to reinforce the idea.

> ⚠ Make sure that you teach some basic safety rules.
>
> Students must never interfere with mains devices – plugs, sockets or cables.
>
> Thin wires may get very hot. Don't use them for classroom investigations. Batteries are generally safe. A great many 1.5 volt batteries are needed to give an electric shock. Ordinary batteries should never be recharged. Never cut batteries open. They are full of chemicals – some of which are corrosive and could be harmful. Rechargeable batteries are useful but have some pitfalls. They can be used again and again, of course. But they may give out a strong current if allowed to discharge quickly – through a short circuit, for example. Don't mix different types of battery.
>
> Advise students against squeezing light bulbs hard or screwing them too tightly into the bulb holders. They are strong but occasionally break.
>
> Remind students that it is never safe to touch live wires from the mains.
>
> Talk about being safe around electricity outside the home, too. Tell students that they should never enter power stations, sub-stations and transformers. Nor should they climb pylons, or fly kites or model aeroplanes or anything that

69

⚠ **continued**

might get close to the cables of a pylon. Warn them of the dangers of electricity near train tracks, too. Emphasize that large electric currents can jump gaps. You don't need to touch them to be killed.

Talk about how the vast majority of people in the world are reliant on electricity and that it should not be wasted. Encourage students not to waste electricity by remembering to turn off appliances when they are no longer needed. Point out to them that this not only saves money by reducing electricity bills, but is also better for the environment. Talk about the importance of being responsible and using electricity safely. Consider developing countries where many people do not have electricity. What might that be like? Talk about what life would be like without television, radio, hairdryers, toasters. How would students manage? What would they use instead?

Language

appliance	something powered by electricity
battery	chemical device that pushes electricity around a circuit
break	(in a circuit) creating a gap in a complete circuit so electricity cannot flow over the gap
bulb holder	a component in a circuit which secures a small bulb
buzzer	a component that vibrates noisily
circuit	path of electricity from the battery and back again
*conductor	a material that allows electricity to travel though it
*insulator	a material that slows or stops the flow of electricity through it
light bulb	a glass container that holds gas and a fine wire (filament) that glows when electricity passes through it
mains electricity	powerful electricity generated in a power station

switch	a means of creating a gap in an electrical circuit
wire	lengths of fine metal inside a flexible insulating tube that allow electricity to pass through

(*technical definitions generally for teachers, not students, at this stage)

The key words to learn are given in the Words to learn list on page 41 of the *Student Book*.

Resources

- *Using Electricity* Reader
- Circuit components: batteries; bells; bulbs; bulb holders; buzzers; conductors; crocodile clips; insulators; motors; switches; wires
- Collection of electrical appliances (and pictures of same)
- Catalogues of electrical appliances
- Card
- Cardboard tubes
- Sticky tape
- Paints
- Glue
- Cardboard box
- Doll's house furniture
- Play people
- Digital camera
- A variety of torches

Bright ideas

Use a hand lens to examine the filament in an incandescent light bulb. Emphasize to students that this is a wire through which the electricity flows and note that it enters the bulb at one point and leaves it at another.

Make up 'Apprentice Electrician' toolboxes using inexpensive plastic toolboxes filled with everything needed to construct circuits. Allow students to role-play electricians with 'job sheets' and diagrams of broken or faulty circuits to fix.

Other investigations you might like to try include:

How does the size of the bulb affect the amount of heat produced?

How is the brightness of the bulb affected by the number of batteries/length of wire/thickness of wire/ type of wire?

Which electrical appliance uses the most electricity?

How could you 'save' electricity at home and at school?

How many different kinds of electrical appliances are there in school or in the home?

Where in the local environment (e.g. outside on the street) are electrical appliances used?

How many bulbs can be lit in one circuit?

Knowledge check

- Students will already know that many things we use in the home and school need electricity to make them work. They may also recognize that electricity can make different things happen such as making a bulb light up or a buzzer sound.

- Students should know that both batteries and mains supply us with electricity and understand that mains electricity can be very dangerous.

Skills check

Students need to:

- think about what they expect to happen in investigative work.

- consider whether their results support their predication.

- make simple observations and offer simple explanations.

- offer simple explanations and conclusions to explain what they have found out.

- identify simple patterns.

- use comparative language such as bright, brighter, brightest.

Links to other subjects

Literacy: Read poems about electricity.

Give students leaflets about safety and electricity to illustrate how leaflets are set out and what they do.

Display electricity safety posters around the classroom to model posters that students could make.

Let students write their own instructions for creating or checking simple circuits and create their own electricity picture stories, using words and pictures.

Encourage students to learn how to spell the key scientific words relating to electricity, possibly as homework.

Create a class big book telling the story of 'The Blackout.'

Numeracy: Look at the numbers on batteries and compare them to the numbers on bulbs.

Create tally charts on how many students and their families use certain electrical appliances during a day, for example toaster, kettle, light, computer, radio and television. Transfer this data to a bar chart and encourage students to ask questions about the data, such as: *Which appliance is used the most?*

Other subjects: In **Design and Technology** students could design and make models that include a working circuit, e.g. a car with headlights, a lighthouse, doll's house.

Let's find out...

The Unit opens with this question:

If there were no electricity, what would not work in our homes?

This question can be used to explore the students' prior knowledge of how there are two sorts of electricity that we use: mains electricity and battery electricity. Students should be able to identify examples of common household appliances that use either battery or mains, or both. You can extend this discussion to cover the impact of electrical technologies on our daily lives by considering what we would have to do without if there was no electricity.

71

Unit 4: Electricity – Bright sparks

The objectives for this lesson are that students should be able to:

- Classify electrical appliances

- Learn that electricity can make things move, light up, heat up and produce sound

- Know that some appliances in our homes use mains electricity

- Know that some things in our homes use batteries

- Understand that mains electricity can be dangerous and understand how to control the risks to themselves and others.

SB p.42 | **Starter**

Look at the *Student Book* page 42. Show the pictures of electrical appliances – some use mains electricity, others use batteries and some use both. *What kind of things use electricity? What can electricity be used for? Which things around the home use electricity? Where do you think electricity comes from? Is electricity safe or dangerous? Why?*

Write students' ideas as a series of statements in thought bubbles and display them around the classroom.

Introduce Michael Faraday, the man most responsible for developing our understanding of electricity. *How old is the light bulb? How many different kinds of light bulbs are there? Where are they used and why?*

SB pp.42–43 | **Explain** | **WS 31**

How does it work?

It is often difficult to explain to young students exactly how electricity 'works'. Electricity is not visible but its effects are and we need to focus on this. At this stage students do not need to understand the movement of electrons in wires (they will come to that much later) but only to recognize that electricity exists and what it can do.

They should recognize that we use electricity in different ways to achieve different things and that some things use batteries and others mains electricity. In daily life we use the term 'battery', but scientists use the term 'cell' for a single cylindrical 'battery'. At some stage, primary students should be introduced to 'cell'. Students can draw examples of things which use batteries and mains electricity on WS31.

Look out for an understanding that even appliances that appear to have only one wire are in a complete circuit. Children often think that because something is 'plugged into a wall' with one wire that the electricity only flows one way. As the Unit progresses, students will come to an understanding of how a circuit needs to be complete for electricity to flow though it. Emphasize this idea throughout.

> ⚠ Discuss issues relating to being safe around electricity.
>
> Never cut open batteries. Avoid rechargeable batteries for school use.
>
> Study pictures of domestic scenes to spot electrical devices. Talk about what makes them safe; the way that the wires are plastic-covered, the sockets protected and even the prongs of the plugs sheathed.

WS31, 32 and 33 highlight the importance of electricity and offer opportunities to discuss electrical safety.

Things to do | **WS 32** | **WS 33**

Around the house

Make a booklet for each student with a labelled page for each different room in the house, e.g. living room, kitchen, bathroom, bedroom and garage. For each page, ask students either to draw or cut out pictures from catalogues of electrical appliances that are used in that room.

Develop this idea into a whole class activity. Display a large cross-section of a house and let students add pictures of appliances to each room.

Produce lots of icons of electrical components. In their booklets, ask students to stick a small battery icon next to pictures of appliances that use battery power and a bulb icon next to those that use mains electricity; some appliances will require both icons. Do a couple together to give students the idea.

Talk about appliances that use mains and battery-powered electricity and why. Discuss related safety issues.

Ask students to give you facts about electricity at home. For example, 'Some appliances like a washing machine are big, and use a lot of electricity so they have to be plugged into a socket.'

What other things use batteries? Ask students to list all the possibilities: torches, remote controls, smoke alarms, toys, portable music systems and radios, hearing aids, watches and clocks. Ask students to complete WS32 and WS33.

Discuss how important electricity is to us. Extend this to consider other places such as hospitals, airports, shops.

Differentiation

Some students will be able to create their own booklets and write the appliances for each room in a list. They will also be able to create their own thought bubbles to explain why some appliances use batteries whilst others use mains electricity. They should also be able to suggest why some appliances use both.

Less able students should attempt only one or two items.

Dig deeper

Batteries come in all shapes and sizes. Usually you will see a figure (multiples of 1.5) followed by a letter V. This stands for volts which is the force of the electrical current.

You may also find letters such as A, AA or AAA which specify the size of the battery.

Did you know?

Lightning is a discharge of electricity in the atmosphere. Lightning bolts can travel at around 210,000 kph (130,000 mph), while reaching nearly 30,000 °C (54,000 °F) in temperature. A bolt of lightning can measure up to three million (3,000,000) volts, and it lasts less than one second!

I wonder...

American scientist and later president of the USA Benjamin Franklin didn't discover electricity, but he did prove that lightning is a form of electrical energy. In the 18th century, Franklin carried out extensive research on electricity. Amongst his many discoveries was the invention of the lightning rod. Lightning rods protect buildings

in the event of lightning by conducting lightning strikes through a grounded wire.

Electricity always travels to the ground. It takes the shortest route whenever it can. If something that conducts electricity, e.g. you, or a tall building, gives electricity an easy path to the ground it will take it.

Other ideas WS 34 WS 35

Invite students to write a story about a fantasy character, and include as many electrical appliances and gadgets as possible that they might use, e.g. rotating shelves in cupboards, a moving walkway in the garden, a shoe cleaning machine, etc.

On large sheets of paper, let students write a story with electrical appliances drawn as pictures instead of in words. Display them. Can other students read the stories?

Study pictures of domestic scenes to spot electrical devices. Talk about what makes them safe; the way that the wires are plastic-covered, the sockets protected and even the prongs of the plugs sheathed. Refer to the picture on WS34.

Together, make a list of all of the electrical appliances that you use during a day. Position it so that students can add to it on a daily basis.

Ask students to design an electrical robot to do something that they don't like doing. They should write about what it does and how it works, and draw a picture, on WS35.

Presentation

Make a collection of objects that use electricity (battery powered is safest) to display on your discovery table. Make sure that the objects are safe for students to handle and use.

Plenary

Refer to your lists of electrical items and their usage that you have been collating. Recap that some items use mains electricity and some use battery electricity. Ask if the students can think of a way of representing this information in another way (a graph, chart, pictogram). *What conclusions can we draw from the data we have collected here? Which is our most important electrical appliance; which do we use the least?*

73

Unit 4: Electricity – What is a circuit?

The objectives for this lesson are that students should be able to:

- Investigate what makes a circuit

- Identify common electrical components

- Create a complete circuit containing a bulb, wires and a battery

- Explain what happens in a circuit

- Predict what will happen when changes are made in a circuit

- Find out what happens when we add bulbs to a circuit.

Starter
SB p.44

Use a large clear light bulb and hand lenses and point out the internal structure of the bulb. Emphasize that a circuit is a continuous pathway and that electricity travels **through** the bulb not **to** the bulb.

The challenge
SB pp.44–45

Tell students that they are going to make a bulb light up. First of all, explain some simple rules:

- Keep all equipment on the table so that it doesn't get lost.

- Don't leave bulbs on for more than one minute because the batteries won't last very long.

Show students the different components and give them the correct scientific name for each one: battery, wires, crocodile clips, bulbs (also known as lamps) and bulb holders. Demonstrate the different terminals of a battery and point out the voltage. Allow students to examine the components and make a circuit.

> ⚠ Tell students not to squeeze bulbs. Dispose of broken bulbs carefully.
>
> Remind them that this is 'safe' electricity and never to play with mains appliances.

What to do

With students in small groups, give each group the necessary materials to make a circuit. Ask them to light a bulb. How many different ways or combinations of components can they find to successfully make the bulb light? *What is the fewest number of wires you need?* While they are working, stop the students at regular intervals and ask them to share what they have found out about batteries and the circuits themselves.

What you need

The number and variety of components can vary. Be sure you have enough so that complete but simple circuits are possible for all groups. Best practice is to allow students to select the materials and components for themselves if possible.

What to check

If a circuit fails to work, look out for breaks in circuits, dead batteries and blown bulbs. Encourage students to work this out for themselves by asking, *What could be broken here?* Encourage students to explain what they are doing. Check connections and tightness of bulbs if their circuits do not work.

Ask students to think about what will happen if they keep putting bulbs in their circuit with one battery. *How could you test this idea?*

At this Grade, students may simply draw a circuit as they see it, without using symbols. Check that the circuit is fully connected in their drawings and that the batteries are drawn the correct way round.

Differentiation

Create challenges suitable for students' different abilities. It may be better to give some students fewer tasks, while others could be asked to classify conductors and insulators.

Ask more able students to light a bulb with two wires and a battery, but no bulb holder. It is necessary to put one wire to the button at the base of the bulb, and the other to the Edison screw. They could also explore switches.

What did you find?

WS 36   WS 37

Encourage students to show their different circuits, with one, two, three and more bulbs. *What happens when you add more bulbs?* Students should remark that after three bulbs or so, the bulbs will not light up at all, although electricity is still flowing in the circuit, as the bulb filaments act like any thin wire.

Ask students to show their picture circuits and discuss some of the problems they had to solve to get the circuits to work.

Are students able to connect components correctly to make a circuit? Can they explain why they have arranged components in a particular way, using scientific vocabulary?

Can students think of different ways to make the bulbs brighter? *What happens when there is a gap in the circuit? Which materials could you use in the gap to make the bulb light? Why?*

Discuss the circuits on WS36 and WS37, and ask the students to complete the exercises. Students will quickly discover that not all materials conduct electricity. There is no need to introduce the words 'conductor' and 'insulator' at this level.

Can you do better?

If the students have followed what the children did and added bulbs and wires to their circuits repeatedly, they should notice that the brightness of the bulbs will become weaker – more able students will perhaps notice that although the bulbs are dimmer, they are all of equal brightness

or dimness and that the bulb nearest the battery is no brighter than any other.

Now predict

Adding another battery to the circuit will make the bulbs shine more brightly. Adding more bulbs and wires to this circuit will eventually result in the same result as before, i.e. the more bulbs added, the dimmer they will all become.

Record

Ask students to draw an A4-sized picture of something that needs a light, for example a car with headlights, a street lamp, a building with a light in the window. Once the picture is drawn, students should make a hole in the paper where the light should be. They should then position their circuit behind the picture and put the bulb through the hole. Make one first to model the idea.

Presentation

On your discovery table set out all the components needed to make a complete circuit – allow students to play, explore and make their own circuits using a variety of materials and components.

Plenary

Create a new set of speech bubbles to add to those from the previous lesson. *What have you found out about making circuits?* Write down and add their responses to the display.

Unit 4: Electricity -- What? No electricity?

The objectives for this lesson are that students should be able to:

- Know that common household appliances use electricity to do different things

- Know that some appliances in our homes use mains electricity

- Understand the impact that electricity has on daily life and that electricity can make our lives easier

- Recognize that electricity can be dangerous

- Ask questions and decide how they might find an answer to them

- Communicate a variety of ideas.

SB p.46 | *Starter*

Use pictures in the *Student Book* on page 46 to discuss a blackout at home.

Ask students to imagine life without electricity for a day. What would happen if the radio alarm did not go off/there was no hot water/they could not have toast for breakfast/all the traffic lights were off?

SB pp.46–47 | *Explain*

What if?

Modern society relies heavily on the convenience and versatility of electricity.

Ask students to imagine what happens during the blackout. *What are the alternatives to the lights, the cooker, the electric fire, the air conditioning unit and the television?* Remind them that battery-operated devices, such as torches and the radio, will still work, as will gas devices such as fires and cookers.

Past times

Discuss what it would be like to live without electricity for a long time and consider parts of the world where there is no electricity. How well could you cope with everyday life? Ask students questions like: *What would happen if we had no washing machines? How would we get our clothes clean? How could we fill our leisure time if there were no television or computer? What would we do*

if there were no electric lights? How would we see at night?

Who lives without electricity today? Is there anyone? Even people who follow nomadic lifestyles can have satellite technology, generators and wind-up radios.

Things to do WS 38 WS 39

Your daily diary

Let students compile a diary of a typical day using WS38 and WS39, noting down what they did and which electrical appliances they used during four separate time periods. For example: 7.30 Got up, switched the light on; 8.00 turned on my radio; 9.00 Turned on the computer in our classroom, etc. Discuss the importance of electricity.

Saving electricity

Talk about where electricity comes from. *How does it get to our homes? How far does it travel?*

The world's biggest source of energy for producing electricity comes from coal. The burning of coal in furnaces heats water until it becomes steam which then spins turbines attached to generators. Coal is a natural resource that could become scarce as we use it up. Ask students to research other ways of producing electricity, e.g. hydropower, wind generation, solar power.

Electricity costs money but also natural resources. Design a poster encouraging sensible use of electricity and cutting down on waste energy.

Differentiation

Let all students create a poster or a leaflet aimed at elderly people, or people with very young children.

Ask more able students to think about the consequences of a power cut for establishments such as a hospital, airport or a shopping centre. *What precautions should be taken in the event of a power cut?*

Dig deeper

This activity is designed to show that not all uses of electricity are the same or take the same amounts of electricity to complete. In most homes refrigerators and air conditioning units use the most electricity of all appliances as they are in constant use.

Did you know?

This is an opportunity to research the different scientists and engineers associated with the development of electricity. Thomas Edison and Joseph Swan came to much the same conclusions about the construction of the filament bulb.

I wonder...

Students can investigate how electricity is generated and how it reaches their houses. Most electricity is generated in power plants either by using coal to heat water to produce steam which then drives turbines to produce electricity; or by wind, hydroelectric, solar or geothermal energy. For example, the Three Gorges Dam in China is the world's largest hydroelectric plant. Hydropower generates electricity by harnessing the gravitational force of moving water (just as waterwheels did in the past). Most hydroelectric power stations use water held in dams to drive turbines and generators which turn mechanical energy into electrical energy. Some countries, such as Norway, Canada, Brazil, New Zealand, Paraguay, Venezuela and Switzerland, produce the majority of their electricity through hydropower – how is yours produced?

Other ideas

Ask students to create a 'story board' to help them plan their own version of 'The day the electricity failed'. Rather than give them the whole day to write about, give different students different parts of the day, for example getting up time, being at school, lunchtime (with cold food), being at home after school, or just before bedtime.

With the story boards drafted, let students create their story, either in prose or as a picture story with captions or sentences. Encourage them to use scientific vocabulary such as power, electrical appliances etc.

Let students create a safety poster warning of the dangers and consequences of playing with electricity. They could include plugs, pylons and being close to electric fires or kettles. Emphasize that electricity can be dangerous.

Presentation

Working together, students can make a public information film on using electricity safely. Use flip cameras which plug directly into your computer or role-play a news broadcast directly to the rest of the class.

Plenary

Look at the poster ideas that students have created. Talk about the safety issues of playing near or with electricity but be sure to emphasize the positive points too.

Unit 4: Electricity – Making models

The objectives for this lesson are that students should be able to:

- Know that bells, buzzers, motors and bulbs are all electrical components

- Understand that circuits can contain different components

- Make models that contain circuits

- Solve problems when working with circuits

- Understand what a switch is and does

- Incorporate switches into circuits.

SB p.48   *Starter*

The child in the *Student Book* on page 48 is having problems trying to make a model using different components. *What are the different components? How could they be used in a model? Does he have all he needs? What else might he use?* (a screwdriver, crocodile clips for good connections). *Could you do the task? How would you do it? What would you need?* Produce the objects, one by one, and ensure that students know the use and function of each.

Play a game of 'hangman' using new vocabulary to familiarize students with the names and spellings of electrical components.

SB pp.48–49   *The challenge*

Tell the students that they are going to find out how different components work and then use them to create their own model or picture. Ask what kind of things they could create, for example: a lighthouse with a flashing light, a car with two headlights or a wheel that goes around, a light in a doll's house room, a picture of a bicycle with a wheel going round, a picture of a door with a bell that works, and a choice card with questions and answers about electricity.

What to do   WS 40

Students need to draw a plan of their model on WS40 before they construct it. They should attempt to show where the circuit will be incorporated and how many of each component they will need.

What you need

Ensure there are sufficient components for all students to use.

⚠ Take the usual care with modelling tools, especially sharp-edged tools. Refer to your school's advice on the use of low-melt glue guns, if used.

What to check

Revisit the criteria to check if a circuit is not working. *Is the battery connected correctly? Are components screwed down tightly? Is there an unbroken path for the electricity to travel along, etc.*

Look out for problems with buzzers. Buzzers usually only work one way, so the wires need to be connected correctly. Only the buzzer will work when a buzzer and a bulb are in the same circuit (the bulb becomes 'another wire').

Differentiation

More able students can be encouraged to explore more complex circuits and make them work.

Support less able students with extra time or adult help to complete their models. As additional support give the less able a 'troubleshooting' list (could be done pictorially) for things to check when a circuit does not work.

What did you find?

Give students components such as buzzers, bells, motors and bulbs and let them explore and make circuits. Once they are confident of placing them in a circuit, ask them to use the materials provided to make a switch, or to use manufactured switches in their circuit so that they can control whether the component is on or off.

Then ask students to create a picture or make a model where one of the components is used (or two if the circuit will allow). They must be able to switch the component on and off so a switch is an essential part.

Use the circuits in other models.

Can you do better?

Talk about switches in the home and why they are used. Students might suggest that a switch

Heinemann Explore Science

is for safety, e.g. an electric fire should not be left on where there are toddlers and no adults. Discuss that switching off an appliance when it is not being used means that we are not wasting electricity and our electricity bills will be lower.

Now predict

Ask students to divide their switch collection into different kinds: those that stay on – like a television; those that you need to hold – like a doorbell or an electric drill; those that you turn up and down – like volume controls and dimmers. Imagine the switches were swapped around – *what would happen?* Discuss having to hold the television on or the doorbell constantly ringing.

Record

Let students write a set of instructions for creating their model or picture, or for checking for faults if a circuit does not work.

Encourage students to take digital photographs of their model or picture and annotate them with captions relating to the components used, any problems they encountered and how they were solved, and hints and tips for making the picture or model.

Presentation

Students have been working to produce electrical models and pictures. Once completed, these will make an attractive display. Encourage students to write captions for their models and display alongside their original designs and diagrams.

Plenary

Invite students to show their working pictures and models. Discuss any problems and how they were solved. Encourage students to be a critical friend and make positive comments on others' work. How could they improve their model or moving picture? For example, by hiding the wires so none can be seen.

Let students show and explain how their circuits work. Can they explain problems they had making their circuits? How did they solve them? Do students use appropriate scientific vocabulary in their descriptions?

Unit 4: Electricity – Circuit pictures

The objectives for this lesson are that students should be able to:

- Know that sometimes circuits do not work
- Know that an electrical circuit will not work if there is a break in it
- Predict and test ideas about why a circuit is not working
- Make simple comparisons and identify simple patterns, with help
- Draw circuits using pictures.

SB p.50 — *Starter*

Look at each circuit on page 50 of the *Student Book*, one by one. Can students describe and explain each circuit, giving reasons why some work and others do not?

SB pp.50–51 — *Explain*

What's the problem?

Remind students of the earlier activities related to circuits. Make sure they understand that it is the complete circuit – and not where components are placed – that makes it work.

Unbroken

The key learning to promote here is that an electric circuit can only work if there is an unbroken path through which the electricity can flow. We may at some point need to introduce a deliberate break in the circuit to enable us to switch components on or off.

A fun way to physically enact this is to play a party game of 'pass the orange' or 'pass the balloon' where students have to move an orange or balloon around a circle of players without using their hands, At a moment of your deciding, remove one or two students from the circle to emphasize that the gap is too large to bridge and so the 'electricity' which is represented by the orange/balloon cannot pass.

Another way of breaking a circuit is to insert a material into it that does not allow electricity to flow through it – we call these materials insulators.

Examples of insulators include plastics, glass, wood, paper and rubber.

Allow students to experiment incorporating different objects made of conducting or insulating materials into their circuits.

Things to do WS 41 WS 42

Apprentice electrician

Give groups of students a range of circuits or put them all on a special Explore science table. Ask them to work out what is wrong with them. When they have found out, they should put the circuit right, and then put it back as they found it. They can then complete WS41.

Create circuits that do not work and take digital photographs of them. Put them in the 'Spot the Mistake' book. Challenge students to talk through the process and use correct scientific terminology.

Allow students to create circuits where something is wrong, e.g. the wires are not connected to the battery.

A circuit diagram

Ask students to create a circuit, or use one from the picture or model in the previous lesson, and draw a picture of the circuit itself. Their picture should look like a diagram.

Emphasize what is important to show in their pictures – it is more important to draw the circuit accurately than to draw the battery design in detail.

You might extend the teaching and learning by introducing electrical symbols. Explain that symbols are used to identify quickly what something is, without having to go into detail. Discuss how we use other symbols in everyday life, such as on road signs, and ask students to complete WS42. This is not essential learning at Grade 2.

On the board, let students draw a circuit with something wrong. The rest of the class must explain why it is incorrect and how to make the circuit work.

Differentiation

More able students could create a set of symbols and create their circuit pictures using symbols instead of a picture of a bulb, battery, etc.

For less able students, to customize the challenges, some students may need to do them in smaller steps.

Dig deeper

The symbols used for circuit diagrams are international; this is so electricians can see what a circuit is meant to look like if they need to repair it. Most of the electrical circuits used in buildings are much more complicated than those we have devised in school and the circuit diagrams are very detailed.

Did you know?

The touch-sensitive switch is one of the more modern switch developments. Students can research this and its applications or research other types of switches; rocker switches, tilt switches etc.

I wonder...

We have already touched on insulators and conductors of electricity. More able students can take this investigation further and group materials by their ability to conduct electricity. Draw the general conclusion that metals are good conductors, and that a complete circuit of good conductors is needed for electricity to flow.

Discuss safety issues, especially to do with mains electricity, and the reasons why wires and switches are well insulated.

Other ideas

Display a variety of torches to illustrate different ways of looking at circuits. Include a transparent torch which clearly shows how the circuit is completed.

Take apart a torch, or let students do it to see how it works. When they have finished they must put the torch back together again so that it lights up.

Students can make their own torches using simple circuits. A 'skeleton' torch can be made by strapping the components to a piece of wood. This is a lot easier to manipulate than one made by putting the components in a card tube, although the latter is more realistic.

Presentation

Add your 'Spot the Mistake' book to your discovery table together with enough components to make a working version of your circuit.

Plenary

A fun way to end this session would be to use a 'cosmic ball' (widely available from educational catalogues and Internet sellers) which shows how humans conduct electricity. Hold the ball to complete the human circuit and see it light up as the circle of hands is completed.

Unit 4: Electricity – Attention seekers

The objectives for this lesson are that students should be able to:

- Understand how problems with circuits can be predicted

- Know that circuits can be used for different purposes

- Create working circuits

- Apply knowledge and understanding of circuits in different contexts

- Represent circuits as pictures.

SB p.52 — *Starter*

Play a video clip of a dramatic police car chase from a popular film or TV series. Make sure that the clip has lots of sirens and flashing lights! Ask students how many different uses of electricity (battery or mains) they can spot and what the electricity is used for (making sound, making lights move and flash etc.). Ask the students why they think the police, in this context, use sirens and flashing lights (to be seen and grab attention, act as a warning and so on).

SB pp.52–53 — *Explain*

Look at me!

Ask students to think about where they have seen things used to catch people's attention, such as flashing road signs, doorbells, sirens, flashing lights on emergency vehicles. Brainstorm simple attention-seeking appliances the students could make.

Display a range of electrical items (or pictures of items) that are used to attract people's attention, such as doorbells, burglar alarms and bicycle lights. *What does each one do? How do you think each appliance works?*

> ⚠ Take the usual care with modelling tools, especially sharp-edged ones. Refer to your school's advice on the use of low-melt glue guns, if used.

Things to do

Grab my attention

Talk to students about making their own device to get attention. *What could you make?* Suggestions might include a choice board; a buzzer for attention when they need help or when they can answer a question; a light for attention during quiet moments; a hand that moves when they want something; or a 'traffic light' that a teacher can use to show when they are ready to answer questions (green), when they can be interrupted (amber), and when they are very busy (red). Remind students that while they are deciding what to make, they will need to think about what their device is for; when they would want to use it; what components they will need; and how to make the circuit.

Teach students how to 'troubleshoot'. Are all connections good? Is the battery 'flat'? Are the bulbs working? Is the buzzer connected the right way around?

Encourage them to create a set of instructions for making their own device, either as a leaflet, a simple list, a set of pictures with captions or a series of diagrams with labels showing the different stages.

When their device is complete, let students demonstrate it to the rest of the class. *What do you think the circuit is like?* Invite students to draw a picture of the circuit they have used in their device.

Differentiation

Support students whose circuits or devices do not work by helping them check their circuits logically. Let students produce a 'spot the problem' checklist for others to use to use if their circuit does not work.

Encourage more able students to make more complex devices.

Dig deeper

This encourages students to think of practical and useful applications for their attention-seeking devices.

Some students could make an appliance for another person, for example a buzzer for a blind person, a flashing device for someone who is hearing impaired. They should first consider the challenge for the person before considering what to make.

Encourage students to make a poster or a booklet called 'Using electricity to get your attention'. This should include how electricity is used daily to do just that.

Did you know?

Electric eels can produce strong electric shocks of around 500 volts for both self-defence and hunting.

I wonder...

Wind turbines and wind farms are becoming more popular and here we can investigate this renewable form of energy further. Students should attempt to look at both the positive and negative aspects of generating electricity by wind.

Other ideas

Let students use their finished appliance for the rest of the day or week. Invite another adult into the class to see their appliances in action. Ask the visitor to question students about how they made it and what they have learned about circuits.

Presentation

Present the students' devices, or examples of attention-seeking devices you have discussed already, to the class. Which device do the students like best? Ask them to vote for a winner and to explain reasons for their choice.

Plenary

Return to the original thought/speech bubbles about electricity and create new ones with information that they have learned throughout the Unit.

What do you think is the most important thing that you have learned? Why is electricity so important? Name four electrical appliances that you think you could not live without. What do you think your doctor/a shopkeeper would choose?

Unit 4: Electricity – Unit 4 Review

The objectives for this lesson are that students should be able to:

- Check what they have learned about electricity in this Unit

- Find out how they are working within the Grade 2 level.

SB p.54 **Expectations**

Students working towards Grade 2 level will:

- Distinguish between those common appliances that use batteries and those that use mains electricity

- Construct simple circuits

- Explain why some circuits work and others do not

- Compare findings with expectations, e.g. 'I thought the bulb would be brighter with more batteries!'.

In addition, students working within Grade 2 level will:

- Describe the dangers associated with mains electricity

- Identify common electrical components

- Construct working circuits

- Incorporate switches into circuits

- With help, identify a pattern in the results such as 'the more cells there were, the brighter the bulb was'

- Use a variety of ways to present what they found out.

Further to this, students working beyond Grade 2 level will also:

- Recognize that components in a series circuit need to be 'matched' if they are all to work

- Represent working circuits in drawings and make circuits from drawings provided

- Make predictions such as 'the more cells there are, the brighter the bulb will be because there will be more electricity'

- Link their conclusions to scientific ideas, e.g. 'the bulb was brighter with more cells because there was more electricity'.

84

Heinemann Explore Science

Check-up

Discuss what Sunil should do to find out why his torch is not working. This question is designed to explore the students' understanding of the various components that make up an electrical circuit.

Sunil would need to check:

- whether the batteries were inserted correctly

- whether there were breaks in the wires or if the bulb had blown.

Throughout this Unit, students should be taught to check components systematically to ensure that they can 'troubleshoot' when a circuit has failed.

Assessment   WS 43

Use the Unit 4 Assessment on WS43 to check students' understanding of the content of the Unit. The answers are given opposite.

Name: _____ Date: _____

WS 43 **Unit 4 assessment**

1 Write three things that use mains electricity.

_____
_____
_____

2 Write three things that use a battery.

_____
_____
_____

3 Look at the circuit pictures.
Tick (✓) which circuits will work.

4 Draw a picture of a complete circuit with a bulb and a switch.

Unit 4: Electricity   43

Answers

1   Three appliances that use mains electricity listed.

2   Three appliances that use battery power listed.

3   Second and third circuits ticked.

4   Accept diagrams appropriate to the level of the students. The circuit must be complete.

The answer!

Refer back to the original question about a power cut. This question is designed to show how we as humans rely on electricity in all its forms in our daily lives. By the end of this Unit, students should be able to name appliances that work using electricity (and or batteries) and have some understanding of what could and could not be substituted if there was no electricity, e.g. we could not watch television but we could provide light without electricity, e.g. by candle light.

And finally...

Students will have discovered that lots of household appliances can be run from battery electricity – but so too can lots of toys and games. Have a 'toys afternoon' where you can provide or students can bring in toys and games that are powered by electricity. Students can also have a go at making a battery-powered quiz game or a battery-powered steady hand game.

Unit 5: Earth and beyond

The objectives for this Unit are that students should be able to:

- Explore how the Sun appears to move during the day and how shadows change.

- Model how the spin of the Earth leads to day and night.

- Use simple secondary sources.

- Make simple measurements.

- Review and explain what happened.

SB
p.55
Science background

This Unit develops students' understanding of the solar system: the Earth, the Moon and the planets within our solar system. More information than you need is offered here, both for background and to meet the needs of knowledgeable students.

Students learn about the shapes and relative sizes of the Earth, Sun and Moon. Using models they learn how the three bodies move relative to each other and how these movements relate to night and day. Experimental and investigative work focuses on making observations and recognizing patterns in first-hand and secondary data. Work in this Unit offers opportunities for students to relate scientific knowledge and understanding to familiar phenomena, e.g. day length, year length, and to consider scientific evidence about the Earth, Sun and Moon.

All around us, huge distances away, there are other spheres; some are planets, some are stars. Collections of stars are called galaxies; ours is called the Milky Way. The most important object to us is our Sun, which is also our nearest star. The closest to us is our own satellite, the Moon.

The key challenges in this Unit are to counteract the misconception that many children, and for that matter adults, hold that the Sun moves – well that's what it looks like, doesn't it! In fact the Sun does not move; it is stationary at the heart of our solar system. It is the Earth that moves in relation to the Sun.

Day and night

We live on a spherical planet called Earth that is continually spinning and moving through space. Earth not only orbits the Sun but it is spinning on its own axis too. Earth rotates once every day, bringing us into the Sun's light and the daytime, once every 24 hours. When the part of the Earth you are on faces the Sun it is day; when it faces away from the Sun it is night. We orbit the Sun, travelling right round it once every year.

The Earth does not spin upright in its orbit, but is tilted $23\frac{1}{2}°$ to the side. The tilt is always in roughly the same direction, with the North Pole always pointing at the Pole Star.

Days, weeks, months and years

Our calendar is set in relation to the movements of the Earth around the Sun, and the Moon around the Earth. The Earth spins on its axis (an imaginary tilted line through the poles) and also moves in a huge orbit around the Sun. The Moon moves in a smaller orbit around the Earth. A day is the average time taken by the Earth to spin once in relation to the Sun. We split the day into 24 hours, each hour into 60 minutes, and each minute into 60 seconds.

The Moon orbits Earth every month. Because it also rotates once every month, the same side stays facing us. It appears to change in shape because it is lit by the Sun and the size of its shadow changes.

A month was originally the time between one new Moon and the next. The Moon is lit by the Sun shining on it, and the new Moon occurs when the Moon is between the Sun and the Earth, so the side of the Moon that faces us is completely unlit. This happens about every $29\frac{1}{2}$ days. Over time, the definition of a month has changed and we now have 12 months of slightly varying length in one year.

A year is the time taken for the Earth to orbit the Sun once. It is about $365\frac{1}{4}$ days. The length is approximated to an exact number of days by having three years of 365 days, then a 'leap year' of 366.

Sundials and time zones

The only timing devices which measure time directly from the motion of heavenly bodies are sundials, and instruments such as sextants. A sundial casts a shadow on a dial marked in hours. Sun time is usually different from clock time these days as we operate in the modern world in time zones where time is relative to the position of the country. Also, most countries reset their clocks by an hour in summer and because the Earth does not go around the Sun in an exact circle, this causes a clock to read about 30 minutes slower in comparison to a sundial in early November, for example, than it does in early February.

The Earth turns through 360° – a full circle – in a day. It therefore turns 15° in an hour. A time zone is a segment of the Earth's surface 15° wide, except where the borders have been redrawn to include an entire geographical region in one zone. When it is noon in one zone, it is 11 a.m. in the next zone to the west and 1 p.m. in the next to the east. The average width of the hour marks on a sundial is also 15°. The Sun's apparent path through the sky is part of an ellipse – that is, an oval. An ordinary sundial with a flat horizontal dial must have hour marks unequally spaced to take account of this.

Language

asteroid	a rocky body that circles the Sun (most are between Mars and Jupiter)
axis	an imaginary line from pole to pole that the Earth is spinning round
comet	a ball of frozen gas and dust that travels around the Sun. Some of the dust streams out to make a 'tail'
dark	having very little or no light
day	the interval of light between sunrise and sunset
Earth	the planet on which we live
full Moon	when the Moon looks like a complete circle
galaxy	a large group of stars
gnomon	the central stick in a sundial
leap year	a year which has an extra day in it
light	the energy that makes things visible; a source of illumination, e.g. the Sun
mid-day	the time of day when the Sun seems directly overhead in the sky
Milky Way	the galaxy where we find our Sun
moon	a small body that orbits a planet
night	the hours of darkness between sunset and sunrise
orbit	the path that the Earth follows around the Sun. When a planet moves around the Sun, or a moon moves around a planet
planet	a large body that orbits a star
round	having a flat, circular surface, as a disk
shadow	a dark area made by light being blocked
source of light	something which creates light
space	space beyond the atmosphere of the Earth
sphere/spherical	a round shape like a ball
spin	to turn around rapidly
star	a celestial body which releases energy from the nuclear reaction at its core
Sun	the star at the centre of our solar system, our source of light in the day
sundial	an instrument for telling the time using the Sun
sunlight	light from the Sun
sunrise	when the Sun appears above the horizon in the morning
sunset	the time when the Sun appears to descend below the horizon in the evening
Universe	the whole of space and everything it contains
year	the length of time it takes for Earth to orbit the Sun once. A year lasts 365 days

The key words to learn are given in the Words to learn list on page 55 of the *Student Book*.

Resources

- *The Earth and Beyond* Reader
- Video or other secondary sources e.g. photographs of Earth taken from space
- Photographs of Sun, Moon and Earth
- Globe with small object attached
- Secondary sources providing information about earlier ideas of the shape of the Earth
- Selection of spheres of different sizes including a beach ball, pea and beads about $\frac{1}{4}$ size of a pea
- Compass
- Shadow stick
- Torch with powerful beam
- Secondary data about times of sunrise and sunset
- Secondary sources providing information about how the appearance of the Moon changes over a 28-day period

Bright ideas

Thinking about space, the Universe and our place in it can inspire many creative activities. Make a collection of pictures related to space exploration; pictures of planets and stars taken from space telescopes are particularly attractive in displays.

Other classroom investigations you might like to try could be:

- Keeping a Moon diary
- Comparing sunrise and sunset times in different locations
- Comparing hours of sunlight and temperatures in holiday locations using brochures

Knowledge check

- Students will be able to indicate and name the Earth, Sun and Moon and be able to compare their relative sizes. They should be able to use different sizes of spheres to model the positions of the Earth, Sun and Moon.
- Students can recognize that shadows are formed when light is blocked and describe that the length and position of shadows changes throughout the day.
- Students can describe how day and night are caused by the Earth spinning on its own axis.

Skills check

Students need to:

- be able to make careful observations.
- make measurements of length and look for patterns in data they collect.
- be able to use secondary sources and secondary data to answer questions.
- be able to record their findings in tables, drawings and simple graphs.

Links to other subjects

As work on space includes a mixture of science, mathematics, imagination and curiosity there are good cross-subject links including:

Literacy: Investigate creation stories, legends and poems from different cultures on the origins of Earth and the Universe.

Distinguish everyday from scientific language.

Describe similarities and differences.

Write labels, annotate diagrams.

Read myths and legends about the Sun, Moon and stars.

Read and write stories about life on other planets.

Role-play a space expedition.

Write a report from the point of view of an alien visiting Earth.

Numeracy: Use simple measures of length to measure shadows.

Interpret simple graphs showing hours of daylight over the course of a month or year. Investigate large numbers relating to the relative size and distances of planets.

Investigate shapes and orbits.

Investigate time.

Other subjects: The science work on space links to a number of other subjects.

ICT links can be made by searching the Internet or using CD-ROMs. Students can link directly to NASA, space telescopes and the latest pictures from space at http://apod. nasa.gov/apod/astropix.html

Art and Design – Make a lunar landscape with a textured surface built up from modroc or white and grey tissue. Make 3D collages or mobiles of the solar system. Design a space logo for a mission to space.

Music – Compose some 'space music' or listen to music inspired by the planets and stars.

Let's find out...

The Unit opens with this question:

Why is it night in some parts of the Earth when it is day in others?

This question invites the students to consider a real-life example of how the fact that the Earth is spinning on its axis has the effect of creating the conditions we call day and night. They may not have considered that when it is day on one half of the world it is night on the other half. Anjuli lives on the other side of the Earth from her aunt, so she will be in daytime when her aunt is in the night. This leads directly into activities where the spin of the Earth and its effects can be actively modelled.

New International Edition

Unit 5: Earth and beyond – A galaxy far away

The learning in this section goes beyond the Cambridge Curriculum Framework Grade 2 expectations. The planets and the solar system are common knowledge for younger students, and engage and excite them. The objectives for this lesson are that students should be able to:

- Learn that the Earth is a planet
- Learn that the Earth is one of eight planets in the solar system
- Learn that the Sun is a star at the centre of the solar system
- Use secondary sources to find out information
- Describe a model of the solar system.

SB p.56 **Starter**

Begin by showing a picture of the Milky Way. Explain that this is the galaxy where we live. Establish the vocabulary relating to our place in the Universe by constructing an address for an alien to visit. Begin with the school name, the street or district, town or province, country then continent, planet, galaxy and finally 'the Universe'. Establish that the Universe is bigger than anyone can really comprehend.

SB pp.56–57 **Explain** **WS 44**

Our solar family

The solar system is not essential at Grade 2, but it is common knowledge enjoyed by younger students.

Explain that solar is a word that means 'to do with the Sun'. Students will have already encountered facts about the Sun in relation to the Unit on light and dark so may be familiar with some of the facts about the solar system.

Actively model the solar system by finding a large space for the students to work in – either outdoors or in a school hall. Explain that at the very centre of the system is a star, the Sun, a huge ball of burning gas that gives us heat and light. Choose a student to be the Sun and give them a very large ball to hold.

Around the Sun are planets; scientists now think there are eight major planets in our solar system arranged around the Sun at the centre. The four inner planets are known as the terrestrial planets and are made of rock and metal. They are Mercury, Venus, Earth and Mars. The outer planets are much larger and are made up of hydrogen, helium and other gases; they are Jupiter, Saturn, Uranus and Neptune. We call these planets the gas giants.

Science changes as we learn more and in 2008 what was previously a planet, Pluto, was reclassified as a dwarf planet. There are four other dwarf planets: Ceres, Eris, Makemake and Haumea.

There is an asteroid belt which lies between the orbits of Mars and Jupiter. It features a large number of irregular-shaped asteroids.

Each of your students will now represent either a planet, dwarf planet or an asteroid in the asteroid belt. Give them either a ball to hold (try to keep the sizes relatively accurate in relation to the Sun) or pin a picture of the celestial body they represent to their clothing. Arrange them in the right order from the Sun.

Distant stars and planets look tiny to us when in fact they can be much larger than our own planet. Explain this by encouraging students to notice how even very large things (like buildings or planes) can look tiny when seen from far away.

In orbit

Now we have something like our solar system arranged but we know that the planets and asteroids travel around the Sun in a nearly circular path called an orbit. See if the students can move around the Sun to create orbits. *Which planet has the furthest to travel? Which has the smallest orbit?*

For thousands of years, humans were unaware of the solar system and believed that Earth was at the centre of the Universe.

Astronomers such as Alhazen ibn al-Haytham, Nicolaus Copernicus, Galileo Galilei, Johannes Kepler and Isaac Newton helped develop a new model that explained the movement of the planets with the Sun at the centre of the solar system.

Ask students to label the planets on the diagram of our solar system on WS44.

Things to do

Model planets

Make a model of the solar system in your classroom by cutting out circular shapes or making papier mâché versions of the planets. Research facts about each and paint them to resemble the real planets. Hang them in order from the ceiling.

Ask students to find out as much as they can about a planet or star that interests them. Use secondary sources and the Internet to research their chosen planet or star and give a short presentation on each to the rest of the class.

Differentiation

More able students can research the history of astronomy, for example the importance of Arabian and Persian astronomy between the eighth and eleventh centuries. They might note the influence of the Arabic language on the names of some of the most important celestial bodies, e.g. stars like Altair, Aldebaran and astronomical instruments or concepts such as azimuth and almucantar.

Less able students should be given lots of opportunities to read about and model the major planets in the solar system and particularly to become familiar with the idea that the Sun is stationary at the centre with the Earth and other planets moving around it.

Dig deeper

The reclassification of some objects in space as dwarf planets happened relatively recently (2006–2008). Scientists classify space objects according to their size and their behaviour. Dwarf planets are in our solar system, are spherical, orbit the Sun but are in an orbit with lots of similar objects in the same orbit, unlike planets which have their own, clear path.

Did you know?

The fact that Jupiter is the largest planet in the solar system is an example of the hundreds of facts about the Universe that students could research

and gives a sense of the scale of some of the planets.

I wonder...

The terrestrial planets closest to the Sun are made of rock but the outer planets are made of gases.

Other ideas

WS 45

A visit to a planetarium or star lab is a useful enhancement activity for any study of space.

Students can imagine sending a postcard from a distant planet of their choosing, and complete WS45.

Human beings have always looked up and wondered about the stars and the planets in the night sky, but it wasn't until the last century that man was able to leave the Earth and travel to space. Find out about the first missions to the Moon and how Neil Armstrong became the first person to walk upon the surface of the Moon in 1969.

Presentation

Make a daily addition to a planetary display by downloading images from NASA's astronomy picture of the day website at http://apod.nasa.gov/apod/

Plenary

We have already modelled a 'static' model of the solar system showing the ordering and relative distances or the planets and other celestial bodies from the Sun. As a plenary you can recreate this model, outside or in a large space, using students as solar bodies as before but this time allow the students to travel around the Sun in an elliptical orbit. This may take some rehearsing and careful choreography to achieve, but the focus should be that the solar system is a moving thing; you may for example like to draw out the paths of the various orbits on the ground in advance. The Sun of course must remain stationary.

Unit 5: Earth and beyond – Spinning around

The objectives for this lesson are that students should be able to:

- Describe how the Earth travels around the Sun in an orbit

- Know that as it travels the Earth spins

- Understand that in the daytime the Sun casts shadows

- Observe, measure and record how shadows change during the day

- Explain in terms of rotation of the Earth why shadows change

- Explain how the Sun appears to move during the course of a day, from East to West.

SB p.58 — *Starter*

Find a video clip or download an animation which shows time lapse photography of the apparent movement of the Sun across the sky. Humans have tried to explain this in lots of ways over time, such as the Sun being a deity. For example, the world heritage site of the Sun Temple at Konark in Orissa, India, was built to honour the Sun god Surya. In Egyptian mythology, Ra or Re was the Sun god who, like the daily Sun, went through various transformations as he travelled across the sky.

Scientists know now however that the Sun does not move – it is the Earth moving that makes it appear that way.

SB pp.58–59 — *Explain*

What is moving?

It can feel counterintuitive to say that the Sun stays still while we on the Earth move. After all – we can see the Sun change position. Can't we?

Just as the children on the roundabout in the picture in the *Student Book* on page 58 are sitting still, people on Earth feel as if they are still when in fact they are spinning around on Earth at great speed just like the roundabout; the difference is that everything else is spinning too. The Earth, like the roundabout, is rotating.

You can model this by asking your students to stand in one place and start turning around on the

spot; all objects around you appear to be moving. If you walk around an object while also turning around, you are doing what the Earth does in relation to the Sun. We rotate and we also orbit the Sun, so the Sun appears to be constantly moving.

Demonstrate this using torch and globe or even shine a torch at the student's chest as the student turns round. The student will notice that the light comes from a different direction from their point of view, even though the torch (like the Sun) has not moved.

Things to do — WS 46

Shadow stick

This is the beginning of a practical investigation to be completed over two lessons. In the following lesson students will carefully measure the movement of shadows across the course of a day. Here, all that is required is for students to notice that there is a change in length and direction of shadows.

Students could use a shadow stick or they could stand on a chosen spot on the yard and have someone draw around their shadow, then come back at a later time and stand in exactly the same place and draw around the new shadow. They can take photographs and note any differences.

This is a practical investigation to be completed over the course of a day. Place a stick in the ground of an open area which is not overshadowed by buildings – a school playground is ideal. At hourly intervals draw around the shadow the stick casts upon the ground. Take digital pictures of the changing length and direction of the shadow cast on the ground by the stick. Ask students to notice the relative position of the Sun at the time each measurement is taken. It appears to move from East to West.

Students will know that the Sun needs to be behind the object which is casting a shadow for a shadow to be made. Note the different directions of the shadows on the ground and compare these with the position of the Sun.

Remind students that although the Sun appears to move, it is actually the Earth that is moving in relation to the Sun.

Students can then complete WS46.

Indoor shadows

A similar investigation can be completed in a shorter timescale indoors. Using a torch with a strong beam to represent the Sun, stick a pencil in some clay to be your shadow stick. Investigate all of the ways you can use the stick to cast a shadow. *Where does the light source need to be to make a very short shadow? Where does the light source need to be to cast the longest shadow?*

Try to recreate these shadow movements but this time keep the torch still – *what do you need to do to make the shadows change now?*

Differentiation

The concept of the Sun moving across the sky is one that is difficult to contradict in young students. Try to adopt as many active and physical models as you can to embed the idea that it is actually us who are moving and seeing the Sun from different perspectives as the day goes on.

Weaker students may not entirely grasp this concept but it will be revisited later.

Dig deeper

There is a long history of astronomical investigation throughout the history of all cultures. Copernicus is famous for his theory of a solar system with the Sun at the centre and planets moving around it but you could usefully choose any astronomer from any period of history to research. Think about the contributions of more recent scientists such as Subrahmanyan Chandrasekhar who was born in Lahore and won the Nobel Prize for physics for his work on the evolution of stars, or Rakesh Sharma the first Indian astronaut.

Did you know?

Another fact to reinforce is the idea that the Earth is moving through space – extremely fast! We don't feel this movement because we and everything around us is moving at the same speed.

I wonder...

Sunrise and sunset are examples of everyday language obscuring scientific explanations. The Sun does not 'rise' or 'set' but rather the Earth moves in relation to the Sun so that it appears to rise above and set below the horizon each day.

Other ideas

Students could write a song or a rhyme about what they have learned so far about our place in the Universe.

In 1972 and 1973 the 'Pioneer' spacecrafts were launched into space, the first human-built objects to leave our solar system. On them were pictures and messages from Earth to whatever races of creatures they might encounter on their voyages. *Imagine you are sending a probe into deep space. What messages might you send?*

Presentation

If you have the technology, use a static video camera on a time lapse setting to take photographs of how the shadows in your shadow stick investigation change throughout the course of the day. Play these back to create a time lapse film of changing shadows in your environment.

Plenary

Take the role of a famous astronomer such as Galileo or Ptolemy and 'hot seat' in that role, answering questions from your students about your life and discoveries.

Unit 5: Earth and beyond – Moving shadows

The objectives for this lesson are that students should be able to:

- Plan a practical investigation
- Investigate how shadows change during the day
- Make simple measurements
- Make simple recordings and communicate their results
- Describe how shadows change over the course of a day
- Know that we can use changing shadows to tell the time.

SB p.60 | **Starter**

This is an extension of the previous lesson where students noticed that shadows changed at different times of the day. It is worth spending time reinforcing the learning that has been developed previously. Show a range of photographs of shadows that you have taken over time in the school grounds. Where do students think the Sun must be for the shadow to be this length and shape? Recreate using your indoor shadow stick.

SB pp.60–61 | **Explain** | **WS 47**

Dangerous light

There are few opportunities for practical scientific enquiry in this topic. This challenging exercise is one. It goes beyond the requirements of Grade 2.

The challenge that Tamara and Leila face on page 60 of the *Student Book* is a practical one and an extension of the previous classroom work. Students should be reminded of how strong and damaging the Sun can be and how to stay safe in strong sunlight.

Use this as an opportunity to emphasize the planning and recording stages of practical work and allow students to think through what they could do to answer the question. One practical solution which Tamara and Leila came up with was to look at the movement of shadows but there are other solutions. Students should complete WS47 to show Tamara and Leila's results.

The students can then carry out their own practical investigation to be completed over the course of a day. Place a stick in the ground of an open area which is not overshadowed by buildings – a school playground is ideal; at hourly intervals draw around the shadow the stick casts upon the ground; take digital pictures of the changing length and direction of the shadow cast on the ground by the stick. Ask students to notice the relative position of the Sun at the time each measurement is taken.

Students will know that the Sun needs to be behind the object which is casting a shadow for a shadow to be made. Note the different directions of the shadows on the ground and compare these with the position of the Sun. Remind students that although the Sun appears to move, it is actually the Earth that is moving in relation to the Sun.

A different solution to the problem is via the use of a 'Sun Spotter', which is a piece of equipment using mirrors which is designed to reflect an image of the Sun on paper. Students can see the image moving quickly across the paper ground in the same way that the Sun appears to move across the sky. Again, it is important to reinforce that it is us who are moving, not the Sun.

An attractive way of mapping the different positions of the Sun is by sticking 'Sun stickers' or cut-out tissue paper suns on a sunny window. If you have a window in school that faces the Sun, you should be able to demonstrate an arc of stickers across the window as you map the positions every hour.

Things to do

Telling the time

This is a practical application of the shadow stick investigation.

Sundials have a central stick called a gnomon (pronounced no – mon) and a dial with hours marked on it. As the Earth spins, the shadow cast by the gnomon moves around the dial and shows the time.

As the Earth orbits the Sun over the course of a year, the height of the Sun in the sky changes so the gnomon needs to be tilted to make sure the dial is accurate. Students can research Internet sites to discover at what angle the gnomon needs to be set to be accurate at your latitude.

Differentiation

Building and using sundials presupposes a degree of proficiency in telling the time. Less able students can try making a 'human sundial' by marking crosses on the ground where they would need to stand so that their shadow can mark the hours.

Dig deeper

A Persian scientist called Ibn al-Haytham spoke of the 24 hours in the day in the 13th century. In fact the idea of a 24-hour day dates back thousands of years to the ancient Egyptians and Babylonians. Egyptian astronomers divided the night hours into 12 distinct sets of star patterns which were seen over the horizon at roughly hour-long intervals. They divided the day into 12 hours to match, and because they lived near the equator, the days and nights were of roughly equal length throughout the year. Throughout the rest of the world, the 12 'hours' of the day and night were of differing lengths depending upon the season. It wasn't until much later that Ibn al-Haytham suggested the idea of hours of equal length.

Did you know?

Sundials are found all over the world but the earliest we know about dates back 3500 years and was found in Egypt.

I wonder...

Timekeeping today is much more accurate than it was in the past and we demand clocks and watches that measure time to the nearest second or millisecond rather than to the nearest hour. Also, sundials are quite difficult to set accurately because of the tilt of the Earth and the angle of the Sun's rays at different points on the Earth. Most obviously of course, sundials can only function when the Sun is shining and do not work on cloudy days.

Other ideas

Create a display based around the 24 hours of the day and night. Keep a diary over the course of 24 hours – *how do you spend your time?* Build your own sundial or other form of ancient clock such as a water clock.

Presentation

Make a timeline of ways of telling the time. Try to find lots of different pictorial example of sundials both ancient and modern to use.

Plenary

Find a downloadable clip or video on a video streaming website of time lapse photography over the course of a day to show to the students. Get them to explain what they are looking at in terms of the Earth moving and shadows changing.

New International Edition

Unit 5: Earth and beyond – Happy Birthday Earth!

Learning in this section goes beyond the Cambridge Curriculum Framework for Grade 2, but extends more able students and introduces the exciting concept of the Earth year. The objectives for this lesson are that students should be able to:

- Learn that the Earth, Sun are Moon are all spherical

- Identify the Earth, Moon and Sun from drawings due to their different sizes

- Know that the Earth orbits the Sun

- Learn that it takes the Earth one year to orbit the Sun.

SB p.62 | Starter

Does anyone have a birthday today? How often do we have birthdays? Most students will know that birthdays happen once every year on the same date. Show the students a yearly calendar. *How is the calendar divided?* Do they know how many days make up a year? *If it is your birthday today, how many days will you have to wait until your next birthday? How did we decide on 365 days in a year?*

SB pp.62–63 | Explain

The Earth is a sphere

Show some photographs of the Earth from space. Ask the students to describe the shape of the Earth. In photographs the Earth looks like a flat round disk but we know that it isn't flat at all. In the past, sailors believed that the Earth was flat and that if they sailed too far from land they would sail off the edge of the world. Now we know that the Earth is a sphere shaped a bit like a round ball that has been squashed a little at the top and bottom.

We can gather evidence from what we see to help prove that the Earth is a sphere and not flat. For example, when ships sailed away from land, people noticed that the bottom part of the ship disappeared first as the ship sailed further from land. You can demonstrate this using a large ball and model ship. This would not happen if the Earth was flat.

We know now of course that the Earth is a sphere because we have sailed and flown around it and we have put satellites in orbit around the planet.

Things to do | WS 48

What is a year?

We know that the Earth travels around the Sun in a roughly circular path or orbit. Scientists have calculated that it take $365\frac{1}{4}$ days for the Earth to orbit the Sun and return to its original position. We call this time a year. Ask more able students to complete WS48. WS48 goes beyond the requirements of Grade 2.

A long trip

At this level students are not expected to be able to explain how seasons occur, but they can recognize that seasons exist and describe differences between them.

Differentiation

More able students could investigate a year on Earth compared to a year on another planet. The planets take different amounts of time to orbit the Sun so a year on each planet is a different length of time. For example a year on Mercury, being the time it takes to orbit the Sun once, is 87.96 Earth days; on Jupiter a year lasts 11.8 Earth years!

Less able students should look in detail at different types of calendars and reinforce the idea of how the Earth year is made up of days, months and weeks and what constitutes a year.

Dig deeper

The change in seasons happens because the Earth is moving around the Sun. The seasons are more obvious as we move further away from the Equator. Seasons change from summer to winter because the Earth's axis is tilted. When it is summer in the northern hemisphere, the North Pole is tilted towards the Sun. In the winter it is tilted away from the Sun.

Countries that lie within the tropics either side of the Equator have the Sun directly overhead for at least part of the year. They tend to have wet and dry seasons, rather than winter and summer.

A common misconception is that we get seasonal change because the Earth moves further away from the Sun, but in fact we are roughly 93 million miles from the Sun at all times.

I wonder...

As planets differ in their distance from the Sun so also do they differ in the time it takes to orbit the Sun. Mercury, the closest planet to the, Sun orbits the Sun in about 87 Earth days; the planet furthest away, Neptune, takes 164 Earth years to go around the Sun once.

Other ideas

Work out your age on another planet! Find out about conditions on other planets – *could we live there?* Write a story about an expedition to another planet; think about how long it would take to reach it and return. *How long would you be away? How long did it take astronauts to reach the Moon?*

There are many stories and myths about how the Moon came to be. Read the Chinese story of Chang'e who, in an attempt to gain immortality, ended up floating to the Moon where she has stayed ever since. Chang'e features in the Chinese Moon festival that is celebrated in the autumn.

Presentation

In groups, or individually, get students to research space pioneers – these could be scientists, astronauts or even writers of science fiction or TV science programme presenters! Write short biographies of your chosen pioneer or collect pictures and collect them together to make a class book.

Plenary

The seasonal variations in temperature and conditions vary depending on which hemisphere you are in and how close to the Equator you are; however, as a plenary you can explore the differences between the traditional seasons in more detail using images and poetry. If seasons are not so pronounced, write a class poem together detailing some of the things that happen in your country and the life of the student over the course of a year.

Unit 5: Earth and beyond – Night and day

The objectives for this lesson are that students should be able to:

- Learn that the Earth spins on its axis

- Learn that it takes 24 hours to spin round once

- Know that there are 24 hours in one day

- Explain why when it is daylight in one part of the world it is darkness in another.

SB p.64 — Starter

Discuss why humans want to explore the Earth – *why do we want to explore space?* Consider some of the benefits of space exploration (extending experiences and knowledge, spin-off advances in technology etc.) and disadvantages (expensive, dangerous etc.). Talk about the development of the International Space Station and show some of the photographs that have been taken from it.

What does Earth look like from the International Space Station? Show an image of the Earth showing one half illuminated in the light of the Sun and one half in darkness. Can students suggest what this shows?

SB pp.64–65 — Explain

Why do we have day and night?

We have day and night because the Earth rotates. It spins on its axis, the imaginary line passing through the North and South Poles. At any time, half of the spherical Earth faces the Sun; in this part it is daytime and the Earth here is lit by the Sun. The other half of the Earth faces away from the Sun. It receives no light and is in the dark and has night. During the course of a day, any part of the Earth (excepting the poles) can be seen to move into the light of the Sun in the morning and out of the Sun's light in the night time as the day ends.

Things to do — WS 49

Make a day

First model the spin of the Earth on its axis using a globe. Students understand that the Earth makes a complete turn once each day. Mark your country on the globe and now shine a strong torch beam on the Earth. Notice as the Earth spins how your country at times is in sunlight and at times is in darkness – this spinning of the Earth is what gives us daytime and night time.

Now ask students to form a circle, facing outwards; they should link hands. Using your torch to represent the Sun once again, ask students to slowly walk around in their circle. They will notice that at some times they can see your torch well (day) and at other times they are facing away from the light (night).

Students should then complete WS49.

Differentiation

Physical enactment in different ways can help students to understand the spin of the Earth in relation to the Sun. They should also be introduced to the more conventional diagrammatic representations of how day and night occur, with the Sun's rays being represented as arrows shining on the Earth and illuminating the half of the planet which faces it, the other half being turned away into darkness.

More able students can investigate, using a light and a globe, where day and night occur in different countries, e.g. when it is day in New Zealand, where is it night? More able students should invent challenge questions like this for each other.

Dig deeper

Use your globes to help students explore which countries will be in day when they are in night and vice versa.

Did you know?

As travel in space becomes more accessible, more people are choosing to go there. Space 'tourism' is becoming more popular. For more information visit http://virgingalactic.com

I wonder...

We know that a year on a different planet is a different length to a year on Earth. What about the length of a day? A day is the length of time that it takes a planet to rotate on its axis (360°). A day on Earth takes 24 hours. The planet with the longest day is Venus; a day on Venus takes 243 Earth days. (A day on Venus is longer than its year; a year on Venus takes only 224.7 Earth days.)

The planet with the shortest day is Jupiter; a day on Jupiter only takes 9.8 Earth hours!

Other ideas

Science fiction books and films are very popular and often feature other worlds and alien races.

Imagine you have discovered a new planet. What does it look like? What sorts of animals or plants inhabit your planet? Is there intelligent life there?

Presentation

Get students to imagine our role in space in the next 200 years and to make some artwork to reflect this for display. *Will we be living on other planets? Will we have encountered intelligent life elsewhere in the Universe? What will our spacecraft look like?*

Plenary

Link in with ICT here as a plenary and look at where your school is as viewed from space using Google Earth. Try looking at other landmark locations too.

New International Edition

Unit 5: Earth and beyond – Unit 5 Review

The objectives for this lesson are that students should be able to:

- Check what they have learned about the Earth and beyond in this Unit

- Find out how they are working within the Grade 2 level.

Students working towards Grade 2 level will:

- State that the Earth, Sun and Moon are spherical

- Identify the Earth, Moon and Sun from drawings due to their differences in size

- Describe how shadows change and the Sun appears to move

- Make observations of shadows and record these.

In addition, students working within Grade 2 level will:

- Explain in terms of the rotation of the Earth why shadows change

- Explain how the Sun appears to move during the course of the day

- State that it is daylight in one part of the Earth and darkness in another

- State that the Moon orbits the Earth

- Use simple secondary sources to find out more

- Make simple measurements

- Record results in tables and charts or in pictures

- Explain what was found out.

Further to this, students working beyond Grade 2 level will also:

- Explain that the changes in the appearance of the Moon over a period of 28 days arise from the Moon travelling around the Sun

- Describe the model of the solar system.

Check-up

Discuss how Hassan's model needs to show the relative sizes of the Earth, Sun and Moon in their respective positions and with distances to scale. In fact the beach ball, tennis ball and pea scale is not entirely accurate as the Earth and Moon in relation to the Sun at this scale would be very much smaller, around the size of a very small ball bearing. However, we should see the beach ball (Sun), a large gap then the tennis ball (Earth) and almost touching the pea (Moon).

Assessment

WS 50

Use the Unit 5 Assessment on WS50 to check students' understanding of the content of the Unit. The answers are given opposite.

WS 50 Unit 5 assessment

1 Nabila's little brother is making a model of the Earth, Sun and Moon. He has collected some things.
Draw a line to the best choice.

PE hoop
dinner plate
tennis ball
football
golf ball
paper plate
marble
beach ball

Earth

Sun

Moon

2 Complete the sentences.
Use these words to help you: **East West Sun spins**

The Earth we live on _____ around. This makes it look to us as if the _____ is moving. During the day it seems to move from _____ to _____.

3 How long does it take the Earth to spin once? _____

4 How long does it take the Earth to travel once around the Sun?
_____

Unit 5: Earth and beyond | 51

Answers

1　Tennis ball joined to Earth, beach ball joined to Sun, and marble joined to Moon.

2　Sentences completed correctly:
The Earth we live on <u>spins</u> around. This makes it look to us as if the <u>Sun</u> is moving. During the day it seems to move from <u>East</u> to <u>West</u>.

3　A day.

4　A year.

The answer!

Refer back to the original question about Anjuli's phone call. This question is looking for an appreciation of how day and night occur and that when it is daytime on one 'side' of the Earth then it is night on the opposite side. Therefore, students should have an understanding of the spherical nature of Earth, and an idea of where the various continents are placed, and that the Earth spins around once every 24 hours with each point on the Earth variously moving into and out of the light of the Sun.

And finally...

Many cultures have myths and legends about the creation of the Sun, the Moon, the Earth or the planets. Dedicate an afternoon to exploring different stories about the creation of the solar system or how the planets move, their 'characters' or music and images associated with them. Use these creative responses to inspire your own works of art, poetry or music based around our solar system.

New International Edition